ECOVILLAGES

Jonathan Dawson is a sustainability educator and activist. He has spent much of the last 20 years working in Africa and South Asia, as a researcher, author, project manager and consultant, primarily in the field of small enterprise and community economic development. He lives at the Findhorn ecovillage, where he teaches sustainability studies up to under-graduate level. He is the President of the Global Ecovillage Network (GEN) and Executive Secretary of GEN-Europe.

Schumacher Briefing No. 12

ECOVILLAGES

New Frontiers for Sustainability

This book belongs to
Danielle Tomerlin

Jonathan Dawson

Foreword by Caroline Lucas MEP

published by Green Books
for The Schumacher Society

First published in 2006
by Green Books Ltd
Foxhole, Dartington, Totnes,
Devon TQ9 6EB
www.greenbooks.co.uk

for The Schumacher Society
The CREATE Centre, Smeaton Road,
Bristol BS1 6XN
www.schumacher.org.uk
admin@schumacher.org.uk

Cover design by Rick Lawrence

Printed by MPG Books, Bodmin, Cornwall, UK

Text printed on Corona Natural (100% recycled)
Colour plates printed on Revive Silk (100% recycled)
Covers printed on GreenCoat Velvet (80% recycled)

A catalogue record for this publication
is available from the British Library

ISBN 1 903998 77 8

Contents

Acknowledgements

This Briefing has been made possible through a generous grant on the part of Gaia Trust in Denmark.

I would also like to express my gratitude to all of the many ecovillagers and other friends who, in the midst of all their other activities, have found the time to help me in the researching of this book. This Briefing is dedicated to all of them.

Preface

Several years ago while addressing a public meeting, I was asked: "Which was the first ecovillage?" My initial impulse was to name Sólheimar, the celebrated Icelandic community created in 1931. However, I allowed my mind to soften, to release the specificity of the modern connotations associated with the word ecovillage and to look for something older. "On the shoulders of which wise ancestors are we standing?" I was asking myself. "To what lineages do we belong?"

Eventually, after reflecting on various communitarian initiatives at different moments in history, I plumped for the Celtic Christian monasteries of the sixth, seventh and eighth centuries off the wild Irish and Scottish west coasts: small, decentralised, generally mixed-gender, only occasionally celibate, and dedicated to loving the land, celebrating the sacred and keeping alive the candle of learning in a time of profound darkness across Europe. (I have since learned from reading the intentional communities scholar, Bill Metcalf, that the lineage goes back much further, until at least the fifth century BC.)

My own answer surprised me and, frankly, came as something of a relief. For I had been labouring under the illusion that the future of the entire communities movement was resting on my shoulders, dependent on my ability to wring a further annual grant for GEN-Europe (the Global Ecovillage Network) out of the European Commission. My epiphany was the acknowledgement that the impulse to live in community—and, on occasion, to live in community defined not by kinship but by shared values and mission—goes back into the mists of prehistory. I began to walk a little more carefree on the Earth.

And yet, it is also true that we live at a distinctive and decisive moment in the history of the communities movement. If intentional communities have waxed and waned in their appeal over the centuries, the current era is one of growth and dynamism. It is no surprise that this should be so. We live at a time of severe breakdown in the community fabric in the richer countries of the North, and of unprecedented threat to ecosystems globally. Parallels between the European Dark Ages, when the monasteries overseen by Colomba and Brendan kept alive the light of knowledge, and our own times may not be so fanciful. If this analogy holds good, ecovillages may well have much to offer as our societies seek to find a way of repairing the damage done, and to set a course for living within the limits imposed by our finite planet.

This short book is an attempt to provide an overview of the ecovillage movement and to gauge its actual and potential contribution to the remaking of a more sane, just, equitable and sustainable world. Historical perspective is always of value, especially at moments of crisis like the present. Consequently, I have chosen to begin by attempting to take the long view, locating modern ecovillages within an appropriate historical and cultural context. Chapters 2 and 3 are devoted to a description of principal areas in which ecovillages are active, with best practice case study material drawn from around the world.

Chapter 4 examines the principal challenges faced by ecovillages, while Chapter 5 concludes by looking forward to the great opportunities that lie ahead and some of the changes that ecovillages and governments are likely to need to make if these opportunities are to be realised. There are very few footnotes in the text, as I have left the great majority of references and sources to the Resources section at the end of the book.

For the last several decades, ecovillages have tended to operate in parallel to and more or less independent from local government and other more 'mainstream' bodies. They have derived substantial benefit from their autonomy, and much has been achieved on many fronts. Today, however, in the face of myriad ecological and social crises, mainstream society is crying out for solutions to many of the very problems that ecovillages have been grappling with. The challenge facing the ecovillage movement today is to find creative ways of responding to this hunger and of building bridges to more mainstream organisations and initiatives.

This trend is already underway, and the pages of this book contain many stories of successful partnerships. Much, nonetheless, remains to be done. My hope is that this Schumacher Briefing may shed some light on the path and help prepare the way for the journey that lies before us all.

Foreword

By Dr Caroline Lucas

E. F. Schumacher has inspired today's green movement perhaps more than any other thinker. His legacy includes the excellent Schumacher Briefings, genuine tools for sustainability. Since 1998 they have tackled such topics as sustainable cities and bio-regions, natural health and green energy, bringing the technology and philosophy at the cutting edge of the green movement to life. In this latest contribution to the canon, Jonathan Dawson provides a rigorous examination of ecovillages, the very communities which are trying, testing and developing the solutions to our environmental crises.

The ecovillage movement was born when the ancient idea of intentional communal living met the burgeoning international green movement of the 1960s and 1970s. An ecovillage has been defined as "a human-scale settlement, harmlessly integrated into the natural world in a way that is supportive of healthy human development and can be successfully continued into the indefinite future". In other words, a peaceful, socially just, sustainable community.

And the ecovillage movement is growing, with many such intentional communities in countries as diverse as the UK and Uganda, India and the US. Such villages are homes to the pioneers of a global future, based on sustainable living—those who have decided to stop waiting for society to wake up to looming social and environmental crises, and to do something themselves.

The successful micro-societies Dawson describes are already reaping the benefits of living in a low-carbon, post-consumerist environment: warmer homes, stronger communities, healthier lifestyles—and they are making a difference, politically and symbolically as well as practically.

But the global threats we face—climate change, poverty, disease and war—can only be solved if we scale up the lessons learned from ecovillages to an eco-society built on the same principles of peace, justice and sustainability.

Although the ecovillage movement is becoming more externally focused, engaging more and trying to export its ideas and sustainable solutions to the wider world, the responsibility for delivering a green future must lie with government.

The neo-liberal capitalist model continues to fail us: it delivers divided societies, environmental destruction and a legacy of climate change and the toxic by-products of industrialisation. Our governments must create the framework for us to adopt greener, cleaner lifestyles, sharing the social and ecological benefits of ecovillage living across the whole of society.

A sustainable, peaceful, equitable future is perhaps our only chance of human survival beyond the 21st Century. We face devastation unless we can learn to live lightly, within our planetary means, and choose co-operation over conflict.

This latest Schumacher Briefing tells some of the stories of the communities already trying to do just this. Our challenge now, both within and outside the ecovillage movement, is to externalise this and move sustainable living from the fringes of society to the mainstream. This volume should help us do just that.

April 2006

Caroline Lucas is the Green Party's Principal Speaker and MEP for South-East England.

Chapter 1

Tracing the threads in the ecovillage tapestry

Ecovillages are the newest and most potent kind of intentional community, and in the vanguard of the environmental movement that is sweeping the world, I believe they unite two profound truths: that human life is at its best in small, supportive, healthy communities, and that the only sustainable path for humanity is in the recovery and refinement of traditional community life.—Robert J. Rosenthal, Professor of Philosophy, Hanover College, USA

Ecovillages seem to have burst suddenly onto the scene. The term 'ecovillage' had not even been coined 30 years ago. Today, it proliferates under a dizzying array of guises. A web search on the word 'ecovillage' takes the browser on a journey through the world of intentional communities in the industrialised North, community development projects in the poorer countries of the South, luxury tourist destinations worldwide (the benign nature of whose 'eco' features tends to be dwarfed by the impact of simply getting there), large-scale, developer-led housing projects and education centres (often with little or no associated resident community). This truly is a term that has entered the *zeitgeist*, even if, in the process, it has made sacrifices in terms of clarity of definition.

However, the concept—if not the specific term—has a much longer lineage. The journey towards an understanding of what is meant by the term 'ecovillage' in the current context takes us back to the late 1980s. Most alternative measures of human well-being (alternative, that is, to the conventional measure of money flows as reflected in Gross Domestic Product) show that quality of life in the industrialised world peaked in the mid-1970s and has been going downhill ever since, even while GDP has continued to climb. In parallel, global ecological footprint studies suggest that around the same moment we moved into overshoot, eating into the Earth's natural capital rather than, as previously, living off its naturally and sustainably replenished bounty.

By the late 1980s, the fall in quality of life was tangible. Ozone holes, species extinctions and deforestation pointed up serious problems of resource depletion and environmental degradation. Community integrity was being steamrollered by economic policies favouring mass production and distribution and the free flow of capital across the globe. Meanwhile, increases in the rates of crime, depression, drug abuse and suicide were sure indicators of the growing alienation and *anomie* experienced by many.

The response of governments to these problems was, on the whole, weak. This was the apogee of the Thatcher/Reagan era, and the frontiers of the state were being rolled back. Corporations were growing in power and it was becoming progressively more difficult to find a candidate for political office who dissented from the neo-liberal, growth-through-trade agenda. The environment was relegated to the fringes of debate and the problems of the socially marginalised were to be addressed through trickle-down growth policies.

The political vacuum that resulted stimulated a growth in what has since come to be called civil society. There was a rich profusion of informal, citizens' initiatives and of popular debate and activism outside national parliaments. Seeds were sown that would sprout into the mass popular demonstrations in Seattle, Genoa and beyond. One of the emerging themes of the period was the question of how to address the challenge of living sustainably. With mounting evidence of, on the one hand, progressive ecological and social dislocation and, on the other, limited formal political response to these problems, citizens' groups began to wrestle with the challenge of creating models for sustainable communities.

Two nodes of activism in this field combined to play a catalytic role in the emergence of the modern ecovillage movement. Hildur Jackson is a Danish social activist who had been involved in the emergence of 'cohousing', a model for human settlements in which a number of households cluster together around a 'common house' where members eat communally and where shared resources—laundry, garden tools, play space, etc., depending on the preferences of each individual group—are stored. While this model enjoys some success in both helping to re-build a sense of community and reducing overall levels of consumption as a consequence of a sharing of resources, Hildur and some of her colleagues remained dissatisfied. Their conviction was that a deeper and more far-ranging transformation was needed in how humans live on the Earth than the cohousing model (which generally permits its members to continue to live fairly conventional lifestyles) could deliver. She and her husband, Canadian entrepreneur Ross Jackson, established Gaia Trust and set about seeking to identify leverage points for facilitating the emergence of more radical experiments in low-impact and convivial human settlements.

Meanwhile, on the other side of the Atlantic, Robert and Diane Gilman were using the pages of *In Context* magazine, of which they were joint owners and editors, to explore the emergence of experiments in sustainable community and to showcase the best and brightest examples. In 1990, Gaia Trust engaged the Gilmans to undertake a study of best practice in the field of sustainable community and their report the following year, 'Ecovillages and Sustainable Communities', highlighted international best practice and provided a series of recommendations on how Gaia Trust could have greatest impact in "helping the movement make the transition from the experimentation stage to the take-off stage (and beyond)".

Some twenty-six initiatives were described in the report as "shoulders to stand on" for the movement. These included traditional villages, cohousing communities, alternative communities in both town and country, the Mondragon network of cooperatives, a Nepali permaculture support project and a Philippines-based network for grassroots sustainable development. The report was a bravura effort of synthesis, bringing together a range of contexts and experiences and attempting to draw from them common themes and attributes for the type of communities that could be pioneers in the transition to a truly sustainable society.

The Gilmans' report defined an ecovillage as a

human scale full-featured settlement in which human activities are harmlessly integrated into the natural world in a way that is supportive of healthy human development and can be successfully continued into the indefinite future.

The ecovillage concept as envisioned in the Gilmans' report did not represent some attempt to return to an idealised past. The aim, rather, was to create a new synthesis that would draw on the best of human expertise in treading lightly on the Earth, community-level governance and the application of modern, energy-efficient technologies.

A contrast was drawn between the growing specialisation, gigantism and alienation of mainstream society with "... a human-scale *integration* of functions, so that the ecovillage becomes a comprehensive microcosm of the whole society". Indeed, it is not going too far to say that the ecovillage model was seen as mirroring a transformation in how we understand the world—mirrored in the findings of complexity theory and systems thinking—emphasising the *connections and relationships* between activities, processes and structures. This was seen as permitting the development of a broader understanding of what constitutes sustainable community, with ecovillages as the microcosmic, physical manifestation of a new holistic worldview.

Further, the vision was one of total societal transformation along ecovillage lines: "... a key principle in our definition of ecovillages and sustainable communities is that they be designed so that a fully-functioning society could be mostly comprised of such units."

The report described the nature of the challenges facing ecovillages in six different areas: "integration into the biosystem; built environment; economy; governance; glue (or values); and whole-system challenge." This listing underscores the most distinctive and generous gift of ecovillages to the wider sustainability movement: namely the attempt in the many and multifaceted environments in which ecovillages are active, to design, build and behave in a holistic manner, with the various physical and social technologies integrated into a whole that is greater than the sum of the parts. This is a theme to which we will return repeatedly through this book.

The Gilmans' report formed the centrepiece of a meeting in Denmark in 1991 attended by twenty leading thinkers in the sustainability movement, including Karl-Henrik Robèrt, founder of The Natural Step, and economist David Korten, as well as the Jacksons and the Gilmans. The meeting concluded that what was most urgently required was good examples of what sustainable and convivial communities might look like. It also noted, on the basis of the Gilmans' report, that there were solid grounds for believing that a wave of initiatives exploring just this territory was already gathering steam.

Before turning to explore how the Gaia Trust set about facilitating the development of ecovillages, it is of value to locate the types of initiatives that were being seen as the harbingers of the new age of sustainability in their correct historical and philosophical context. The ecovillage pioneers were looking to the intentional communities movement in the industrialised world as a major source of hope and inspiration. These can be characterised as initiatives generally undertaken by small groups of private citizens to create micro- or small-scale settlements (the Gilmans' report set an upper limit of roughly 500 people on ecovillage settlements), largely independent of governmental support and often seeking to create visionary, alternative modes of community.

Seventeen of the Gilmans' twenty-six 'shoulders to stand on' initiatives can be defined as intentional communities, all but two of which are in the global North; moreover, the two Southern communities—Auroville in India and Aztlan in Mexico—have a significant expatriate, Northern population. At the time of the writing of the report, thirteen of the communities had a population of less than 100 people.

Were such intentional communities a relatively recent phenomenon at the time of the Gilmans' report? Emphatically not. Communities scholar Bill Metcalf reckons that the first intentional community that we would recognise as such today was Homakoeion, developed by Pythagoras in about 525 BC (though he acknowledges that some Biblical scholars consider the eighth-century BC prophet Amos as the first recorded intentional community designer!).

Since then, the intentional communities movement has waxed and waned. Notable moments of waxing included the second century BC, when around 4,000 Essenes lived and worked together in their commune overlooking the Dead Sea; the centuries following Patrick's mission in Ireland when Celtic monasteries flourished; the millenarian communes (including those of the Cathars) of the European Middle Ages; the Diggers of seventeenth-century England; the communal initiatives inspired by Robert Owen's New Lanark; and the eighteenth and nineteenth centuries in many countries of Europe where, according to Metcalf, community builders and dwellers "sought not to retreat into a bucolic, spiritual, non-material world, but envisioned modern intentional communities, using modern technologies, to liberate people from capitalist oppression". The most recent upsurge of interest in intentional communities is in the age in which we live today.

Diverse threads are woven into the fabric of the modern-day intentional communities movement. One important lineage, apparently as old as the movement itself, is the ideal of self-reliance and spiritual enquiry kindled in the world's religious communities This thread is most evident today in communities like the Catholic l'Arche in France and quasi-monastic communities like Plum Village, created in France by the exiled Vietnamese Buddhist monk, Thich Nhat Hanh. However, the spiritual impulse is also deeply embedded in many non-monastic initiatives, including the

Auroville community in India, and among groups that form part of the New Age movement in the North. Among all of these, Gandhian principles of self-reliance, decentralisation and spiritual enquiry remain of paramount importance.

Closely related, and perhaps the most powerful modern manifestation of intentional communalism, is the kibbutz movement in Israel. The kibbutz model offered the creators of the new state the opportunity to marry principles of self-reliance, social justice and nurturing of the cultural and religious values at the heart of Zionism. At the peak of the kibbutz movement, they played home to seven per cent of the population of Israel and provided the heart of the new state's economy.

Many other contemporary threads are also woven into the ecovillage tapestry. The Back to the Land and hippie movements of the 1960s and 1970s represented a rejection by youth of mainstream, materialist values, a yearning for reconnection and the launch of myriad experiments in the re-creation of community in the West. The cohousing movement, launched in Denmark and spreading rapidly internationally, represented a less radical but no less important attempt to create human-scale settlements that tread more lightly on the Earth while offering to their residents a real sense of community.

Many who were active in both the environmental and feminist movements began to see the links between the patriarchal oppression of women and the domination and destruction of the Earth which, like women, was seen as a passive resource to be exploited for profit and which could and would reproduce on demand. The emerging small-scale, egalitarian communities were seen as ideal laboratories for the birthing of a new society, based on ecological principles and in which men and women might co-exist as true equals. In common with several eighteenth- and nineteenth-century experiments, a number of today's intentional communities also experiment with moving beyond what is seen as the repressive, socially sanctioned norm of heterosexual monogamy.

German peaceniks created settlements based on ecological principles (ökodorf—literally 'ecovillage') next to the nuclear plants against which they were protesting, in the process moving beyond rejection of nuclear weapons to being proactively ecological. Meanwhile, treading in the footsteps of Gandhi, E.F. Schumacher proposed the development of intermediate technologies as key to the evolution of more human-scale and community-based societies. His efforts and those of the organisation he created, the Intermediate Technology Development Group (recently renamed Practical Action), were primarily geared to the context of the global South. But his ideas found a growing number of advocates in the North, and decentralised, human-scale technologies emerged as a key element of many of the new community-based experiments.

The alternative education movement provides another important motivation for modern-day communards. Deeply dissatisfied with a state education system primarily designed to train young people as workers and consumers within the industrial growth economy, many created their own models and systems, aiming for a more rounded and holistic approach. Alternative, holistic education continues to be the core activity and largest single source of income for many intentional communities.

The new element that has been the primary driver of the current upsurge in interest in the communities movement has been growing awareness of the seriousness of the ecological problems faced by humanity. The failure of governments to address this crisis in any systematic manner has led people in unprecedented numbers to conclude that the core direction of mainstream society is so fundamentally flawed that it cannot be reformed from within but must, rather, be transcended from without.

Many of those communities that include the need for ecological sustainability at the forefront of their raison d'être, along with social justice, peace and the creation of a human-scale society, are now calling themselves ecovillages. This is such a strong trend that, in the words of Bill Metcalf: "Ecovillages are becoming so popular throughout much of the world that many people imagine them to be the only type of intentional community."

The ecovillage pioneers were not, however, pinning all of their hopes on the resurgent intentional communities movement. For, in a genuinely new and radical departure, the ecovillage concept was also to embrace popular movements in the global South. Several of the ecovillage pioneers had been seeking to build bridges between visionary movements in the North with Southern-based organisations and networks for some time. Hildur Jackson, in her work as co-ordinator of the Nordic Alternative Campaign, had, for example, developed a working relationship with Helena Norberg-Hodge, whose work in Ladakh proved such an inspiration to the pioneers of the modern ecovillage movement.

Other visionaries from the South, or having strong connections with it, were also pulled into the debate on how to shape a global sustainable communities movement. These included Ari Ariyaratne, director of the

Sarvodaya organisation, which works with around 15,000 villages nation-
wide in Sri Lanka; Rashmi Mayur, president of the Global Futures Network
and director of the International Institute for Sustainable Future in India;
Bernard Lecompte of the Naam movement in Burkina Faso, which brings
together almost 700 village groups with a combined membership of
300,000 people; and Indian physicist and activist Vandana Shiva.

Two key common threads were identified which link the Northern
intentional communities and Southern community-based initiatives. First,
both were seeking to consciously regain greater democratic, popular control over community resources that were coming under ever-greater attack
from corporate capitalism. Second, both recognised that at root, the problem to be addressed was at least as much cultural as economic in nature.
That is, in the South, traditional communities were being undermined not
only by the aggressive behaviour of corporations in usurping control over
community resources, but also by the barrage of media messages undermining traditional values and ways of life.

In the North, meanwhile, efforts at self-reliance and restraint were
swamped by the prevalent corporate-driven cultural norm that quality of
life could be equated with levels of material consumption. Movements both
North and South, consequently, defined their objectives equally in terms of
cultural renewal and economic empowerment. Marian Zeitlin, one of the
pioneers of the ecovillage movement in Senegal, put it thus: "In Senegal,
becoming an ecovillage is no less than the act of reclaiming spiritual and
cultural integrity, pride in tradition, heritage of mutual aid, community solidarity, self-reliance and self-respect that first were lost through colonial
conquest."

The vision of the ecovillage pioneers in seeking to effect this marriage
between initiatives and networks North and South was grounded in a radical critique of the whole 'development' paradigm that underlies and indeed
defines post-Enlightenment society. In the place of a linear, developmental
model where stragglers (the Third World) follow on a path defined by the
leaders (the First World) of indefinite growth, the ecovillage philosophy was
based on respect for equality and diversity within the confines of a finite
Earth. This was an especially powerful and welcome message in the South
where, in contrast with conventional developmental thinking, the knowledge and skills of the small-scale farmer and artisan were viewed as
strengths to be built upon rather than a problem to be solved on the fast
track to modernisation.

Momentum developed in the years following the 'Founders' meeting in 1991. In May 1992, Michael Boddington, an Englishman who had worked with Schumacher, was commissioned to prepare a report, 'Technologies for Life, Sustainable Technologies for Ecovillages'. This was instrumental in the creation of the Gaia Trust venture capital company, Gaia Technologies, among whose aims was to pioneer the development of intermediate technologies relevant to the needs of ecovillages North and South.

An intense period of discussions and networking followed. What emerged was a conviction that a wave of community-based, sustainability-related initiatives was growing fast and that it had revolutionary potential to facilitate a change in the very direction of society. New initiatives were also taking off on the ground. Supported by a Gaia Trust grant, the first Ecovillage Training Centre was created at The Farm ecovillage in Tennessee. The Green Kibbutz movement was established, with support from ecovillage activists internationally.

Finally, after four years of consultations, the ecovillage pioneers were ready to launch.

A conference at the Findhorn Foundation in Scotland in 1995 entitled 'Ecovillages and Sustainable Communities: Models for the 21st Century' drew 400 participants from around the world, with a further 300 turned away. Then, at the UN HABITAT conference in Istanbul in 1996, the Global Ecovillage Network (GEN) was launched, as "a global confederation of people and communities that meet and share their ideas, exchange technologies, develop cultural and educational exchanges, directories and newsletters, and are dedicated to restoring the land and living 'sustainable plus' lives by putting more back into the environment than we take out".

GEN's main aim was to encourage the evolution of sustainable settlements across the world, through:

- internal and external communications services;
- facilitating the flow and exchange of information about ecovillages and demonstration sites;
- networking and project coordination in fields related to sustainable settlements; and
- global cooperation and partnerships, especially with the United Nations.

Three regional nodes were created: ENA (the Ecovillage Network of the Americas), GENOA (GEN for Oceania and Asia) and GEN-Europe. GEN-

Europe was also assigned the task of fostering the development of the ecovillage model in Africa and the Middle East. Over the last decade, GEN has been an active player on the international stage and many new ecovillage initiatives have developed on every continent.

Before turning to this story, however, let us look in a little more detail at just what ecovillages look like and the kinds of activities they are involved in. This will be the subject of the next two chapters. Chapter 2 profiles five ecovillage initiatives, in Asia, Africa, Europe, North America and South America. Chapter 3 takes us on a journey of ecovillages worldwide, looking at their activities in a broad range of thematic areas.

Chapter 2

So, what do ecovillages look like? Five case studies

The movement to create ecovillages is perhaps the most comprehensive antidote to dependence on the global economy. Around the world, people are building communities that attempt to get away from the waste, pollution, competition and violence of contemporary life.—Helena Norberg-Hodge, director of the International Society for Ecology & Culture

Ecovillages are heterogeneous to the extent that that no one model covering all cases can be described. The Gilmans' guiding definition, "human scale, full-featured settlements in which human activities are harmlessly integrated into the natural world in a way that is supportive of healthy human development and that can be successfully continued into the indefinite future", is too imprecise to work as a tight definition and is, moreover, more aspirational than descriptive: it points to the goal towards which ecovillages seek to move rather than a state which any has yet achieved.

Nor can membership of the Global Ecovillage Network (GEN) be used as a practical, proxy means of defining what constitutes an ecovillage. For, while GEN defines a large and growing international family of ecovillages, many initiatives lying outside GEN clearly belong within the ecovillage family. Numerous communities in the global South, for example, clearly qualify as ecovillages but exist in countries where GEN is inactive or unknown. Other initiatives have chosen not to join GEN, in some cases because they are already members of pre-existing networking organisations (such as the Fellowship of Intentional Communities and the Federation of Egalitarian Communities in North America), in others because networking is simply a low priority for them.

In this context, the most helpful way forward may be to describe a number of current initiatives and to use these case studies as the basis for a wider discussion of the essence of the ecovillage movement.

Ecovillages, cohousing projects
and developer-led eco-settlements

Before doing so, however, it may throw some light to locate ecovillages in relation to two of their close cousins: developer-led eco-communities and cohousing initiatives. The *developer-led eco-community* is pretty much self-explanatory. It is a more or less conventional housing development, undertaken by an entrepreneur with the ultimate aim of turning a profit, but intentionally designed so as to be as ecologically benign as possible. Residents are selected—or self-select—via the housing market, more or less as they would for any other housing development and, naturally, have no say in the design or construction of the settlement.

There are currently relatively few developer-led eco-communities, but the model is growing in popularity. The most celebrated such project is the Beddington Zero Energy Development (BedZED) in South London, so named because it is designed, in theory at least, to be able to generate as much energy as it consumes. The developer-led model also appears to have some backers in China: a pilot city of 180,000 incorporating sophisticated eco-friendly design features is planned for construction in the next few years in the east of the country.

The *cohousing model* also sees the central developer as having a core role to play: the settlement is generally planned and built as a whole. However, those who will be residents have an important say in determining the design, which tends to have a stronger emphasis on social and community dimensions than with developer-led eco-settlements. Thus, in cohousing, there is always a community house for shared meals and other social functions, although all dwellings are self-contained, meaning residents can choose the level of integration within the community that feels appropriate for them. In addition, and unlike developer-led eco-settlements, residents take full responsibility for self-management of the project once it is occupied, with decision-making tending to be taken on the basis of consensus.[1]

With some notable exceptions, of which more below, cohousing residents participate in the mainstream economy in a fairly conventional way:

---

1. In fact, in many—perhaps most—cohousing settlements, it is only a portion of the residents (those who have been involved in the early stages of the project) who tend to be involved in the design phase. Often, most long-term residents are not identified until after the settlement has been designed and/or built.

most have regular jobs and pay mortgages and there is no pooling of incomes. In the words of cohousing scholar Graham Meltzer, "Cohousing is a *mainstream* option and intentionally so. It is not an 'alternative' lifestyle but one deemed appropriate for the broad majority of people." Cohousing is popular in Denmark, where it originated, Sweden, the Netherlands, the US and Canada. A few projects exist in Australia, New Zealand and Japan and cohousing is beginning to take root in the UK, with the first project recently created in Stroud.

Ecovillages take the social dimension further still and are altogether more radical in their approach. While there is so much diversity within and among ecovillages that generalisations are often difficult to make, broad patterns are identifiable. Ecovillagers not only design their settlements but often also build them: construction companies, often staffed by builders who have learned their skills on the job, proliferate in ecovillages and there is also a strong self-build tradition, using locally available and also sometimes recycled materials. Some ecovillages design and construct or retrofit according to a central plan, but just as often, buildings get built or renovated over time, as money becomes available, and there is often great diversity in building styles.

The community dimension of life in ecovillages is stronger than in cohousing projects: residents have less private space, many more members work within the community (often for wages well below those in the mainstream economy) and a good number have some element of income-sharing or other ways of redistributing economic wealth among the members. Critically, ecovillages tend to be communities of strongly shared values. The nature of the common values differs widely within the ecovillage family, but most draw their inspiration—in different measure according to the focus of each specific ecovillage—from ecological, social, economic and spiritual concerns. Ecovillages tend to see themselves as being in service to a wider cause, generally phrased in terms of ecological restoration, strengthening community, nurturing the local economy and/or deepening spiritual insight. Most are engaged in educational and other demonstration activities as a way of communicating their message and insights to the wider world.

This classification is somewhat confused by the fact that in recent years there has been some blurring of the lines between ecovillages and cohousing projects. This has happened both due to dissatisfaction on the part of some cohousers that their model is insufficiently community-minded or socially and politically radical; and of ecovillages recognising that the cohousing model may offer potential benefits in terms of simplifying the design and building process. This is an important theme that we will return to below.

Five case studies

The case studies that follow do not pretend to be representative of the movement as a whole. They have, nonetheless, been selected to provide a good overview of important themes and trends that exist within the movement. Most ecovillagers will see the core essence of their own community more or less reflected in one or more of these portraits. Their geographical balance—one each from Asia, Africa, Europe, Latin America and North America—is intended to show the global reach of the ecovillage phenomenon.

Auroville, India

Among the best known and most successful ecovillages, Auroville is located near Pondicherry in the state of Tamil Nadu, south India. Arising out of a vision by 'The Mother' (a French woman born as Mira Alfassa who was a co-worker with the Indian sage Sri Aurobindo), it is a self-declared "ideal township devoted to an experiment in human unity". Its population is around 1,700, but its ultimate aim is to become a city of 50,000 people. Aurovillians come from 35 countries and one-third of the population is Indian.

The birth of the community could hardly have been more auspicious: on February 28, 1968, some 5,000 people assembled near the banyan tree at the centre of the future township for an inauguration ceremony attended by representatives of 124 nations, including all the states of India. All of the representatives brought with them some soil from their homeland to symbolically mix with the soils of Auroville. The initiative, moreover, had the endorsement of UNESCO as an experiment in intercultural cooperation and development.

When Auroville was launched, the land was denuded of nearly all vegetation, and frequent wind storms and monsoon deluges stripped it further of its meagre topsoil, carving ravines as rainwater poured down from the plateau into the sea. The first priority of the new settlers was to create dams and dykes to stop the run-off of monsoon floods, and to plant trees. The enthusiasm of the newcomers allied to the indigenous knowledge of the locals proved a winning match and today, almost thirty years on, more than two million trees have been planted, water management programmes have been implemented, and the local ecosystems restored to health.

Initially, there was no electricity in the area, and the early settlers began to install windmills to pump water and generate power. Community businesses worked hard to develop biomass and solar technologies, and today Auroville has the biggest concentration of alternative and appropriate energy systems in India. Of particular interest is the massive 15-metre diameter solar collector installed on the roof of the solar kitchen, designed to generate enough steam to cook up to 1,000 meals a day.

Auroville's farms cover around 135 acres; the community is self-sufficient in milk and produces almost half of its total fruit and vegetable requirements. There is also a seed bank, with a very large collection of tree and vegetable varieties.

Auroville has become an important resource for communities both within its own bioregion and on the Indian sub-continent as a whole. It works with local communities in the cataloguing of medicinal plants and associated seed-saving. Working in partnership with many agencies, it has exported the technologies it has developed to communities across the sub-continent, including 8,700 home-lighting kits and 550 solar water pumps to communities in northern India. In 2003, Auroville won an Ashden Award for Sustainable Energy (the Green Oscar) primarily to mark the community's achievements in reforestation and renewable energy. Its Centre for Scientific Research is an acknowledged centre of excellence for the entire Indian sub-continent.

Auroville's success can be traced to three core factors. First, at the heart of the enterprise is a strong spiritual impulse that acts as powerful community glue. The spiritual guidance provided by Sri Aurobindo and The Mother combine with an ethic of service arising out of the community's location in one of the poorest parts of the world to generate a strong body of shared values within the community. This is most evident in the huge financial and human resources invested in the Matrimandir, the great meditation dome located in the heart of the community, but in fact pervades all the community's work. Second, Auroville's status as a powerful symbol of hope and unity affords it many friends both within India and internationally. This has provided it with a steady stream of willing servants and generous grant funding from individuals and the aid donor community.

Finally, the community has developed a strong economy of solidarity that has served to redistribute financial wealth within the community and to make private monies available for the collective. Those who can afford to invest their savings in the collective body, while forgoing interest payments, are invited to do so. Meanwhile, since 1999, the 'circle system' has been in operation whereby some Aurovillians, generally in groups of around twenty members, share their income in a common pot, seeking ways of balancing out inequalities. All members of the community are entitled to a basic minimum income. These various mechanisms have helped contribute to a flourishing community economy with around 125 enterprises, all owned by the collective, involved in the manufacture and retailing of handicrafts, computers and food, together with building, energy, food and waste-treatment technologies.

Mbam and Faoune, Senegal

Mbam and Faoune are rural communities lying to the south of the Senegalese capital Dakar. The former lies in the Siné-Saloum delta, around 100 kilometres from the capital, while the latter is further south in the Casamance region, just beyond Senegal's southern frontier with Gambia. Both communities, in common with those that surround them, face substantial challenges.

Pivotal to the maintenance of the Siné-Saloum delta's fragile eco-system are the mangrove forests. Unique among land-based plants, the mangrove is able to live in salt water. In fact, the mangrove is so effective as a saline filter that the land immediately behind is largely free from salt. Much of this land in the delta is used to grow rice.

In the mid-1980s, however, a terrible drought hit the entire Sahelian region and the mangroves came under unprecedented threat. In part, this was because the plants were weakened by the extremes of temperature that prevailed. More serious was the impact of migrants from the countries to the north and east that were even more seriously affected than Senegal—especially Mauritania, Mali and Burkina Faso. Villagers in the delta had always harvested wood from the mangroves as cooking fuel. However, the sudden increase in human numbers began to undermine the ability of the trees to self-regenerate. Many of the new arrivals made their income from the sale of fish, for which they needed large quantities of wood for smoking. (Previously, villages such as Mbam had tended to catch just enough fish for local consumption.) Within years, the mangroves were dying and the open sea was pouring into what were once rich paddy fields.

The crisis to hit Faoune and surrounding villages in Casamance had earlier roots. Up until the early years of the twentieth century, most communities had grown a variety of crops, with sesame playing a central role in the village economy. Sesame is useful as a food crop, a cash crop and as a base for medicinal and cosmetic products. However, under pressure from the colonial power, the region became a mass producer of one principal cash crop, peanuts. Relative to sesame, peanuts have numerous disadvantages: they cannot so easily be inter-cropped with food crops; they have no uses other than as a cash crop; they deplete the soil of nutrients and cannot be processed at village level.

In addition to these ecological and economic problems, both Mbam and Faoune, in common with similar communities throughout the countries of the South, find themselves under a form of cultural assault. Television, radio and newspapers alike send a barrage of images and messages glamourising Western, modern, urban life-styles and denigrating their own traditional values. Caught between the pincers of, on the one hand, ecological and economic crisis and, on the other, loss of cultural coherence and self-confidence, the able-bodied young were leaving for the cities.

What singled out Mbam and Faoune from their surrounding communities—and what sets them apart as ecovillages—is that at their heart were groups of citizens with some local power, who recognised the nature of the crisis they faced and who were determined to wrest back greater control over their communities' destiny. Both applied to become ecovillages and went through a process of accreditation designed by the founding members of GEN Senegal. This engages villagers in exploring and scoring their activities in numerous fields—including culture, economy, health and spirituality—and in defining their commitment to becoming locally sustainable.

Today, both these communities have become centres of research, training and demonstration for their surrounding areas. There are three distinctive dimensions to the way in which they have done so—and these, in some measure, set them apart from more conventional development projects. First, the individual communities have remained in the driving seat, choosing the direction and speed of their own process of transformation. Second, through GEN Senegal, they participate in the design and delivery of various technical inputs integrated to provide a holistic package. Finally, recognising the importance of the cultural dimensions of sustainability, these communities place a strong emphasis on preserving, celebrating and sharing their indigenous values, beliefs and customs.

Members of the two villages have participated in training programmes organised by GEN Senegal, including wetlands management and mangrove reforestation, permaculture gardening, internet and computer literacy, eco-tourism and the preparation of proposals for funding opportunities, for which GEN Senegal provides coaching and logistic support. Support in this latter area has helped Mbam win a grant from the Global Environmental Fund for a biogas development project. Mbam has become an important resource for surrounding villages, especially in the organisation of work parties to replant mangroves.

Faoune is today the headquarters of an organisation, COLUFIFA (French acronym that translates as Committee to Put an End to Hunger), which works with 350 villages in Senegal and three neighbouring countries, Gambia, Guinea-Bissau and Guinea-Conakry. COLUFIFA was created by Demba Mansaré, who moved to the area as a student inspired by the teachings of Gandhi, in response to the drought of the 1980s. It has five core objectives: "the promotion of food security, financial autonomy, health for all, training for all and the protection and development of the physical and cultural environment." Its efforts are focused on the reintroduction of sesame production and the promotion of a range of associated activities, although it also promotes other income-generating enterprises, including poultry-raising, bee-keeping, and dry-season vegetable production. There are programmes to promote literacy, dig wells, build houses using local bamboo, research uses of various local plants and promote the use of solar ovens. The COLUFIFA network of villages has developed a strong relationship with several international partner organisations, especially in Denmark.

Sieben Linden, Europe

The German ecovillage Sieben Linden represents an attempt to create a very low-impact human settlement that is woven into the fabric of its own bioregion. The initiators of the project began meeting in 1986 and worked intensively on the establishment of a set of clear goals for the project. Since they wished to build a new settlement, rather than retrofitting an existing one—so as to be able to experiment with self-sufficiency in all areas of life, including closed resource circuits and eco-friendly building techniques—this proved a long and difficult process. Both the existing planning legislation and the difficulty in finding an open-minded village council with enough adjacent land proved formidable obstacles.

Eventually, however, a sympathetic mayor in the village of Poppau in the former East Germany was identified and in 1997, a farm of twenty-two hectares adjacent to the village was purchased. This was made possible through contributions by each of the members (a minimum of €12,000 per head is needed to buy into the ecovillage land cooperative) together with interest-free, long-term loans made by friends of the initiative. The project also benefited from the low land prices prevailing in this part of Germany. Today, the site has grown to forty-four hectares, including twenty-eight hectares of forest.

The immediate need was to renovate the farmhouse using low-energy building standards. This has become the community and visitors' centre. The pioneer group moved onto the land in circus wagons and many of the inhabitants still live in these. The first residential homes were built balancing the need for speed of construction with the community's strict ecological building code. Very high levels of insulation were achieved.

Later buildings have become more radical in both design and construction. One large straw bale house, for example, was built entirely from wood, cob and other products harvested on community land and worked by hand (and foot in the case of the cob!) and horse without the use of any power tools. Other buildings, including the three-storey community house that is the largest straw bale building in Europe, have also been designed to use a maximum of local materials and to require significantly less electricity than conventional homes.

Sieben Linden has been lobbying hard for a change in the building regulations in Germany to make it much easier and cheaper to build with straw bales; to date, all applications to build with this material are considered individually in what is a long and expensive process. A change in legislation along the lines promoted by Sieben Linden is likely to be enacted in the near future.

The community's electricity is generated by photovoltaic panels and power is sold to and bought from the grid. Water is also heated by solar panels. All home heating is provided by wood harvested on community land. Much effort is put into the production of food within the community: it is about seventy-five per cent self-reliant in vegetables, and buys its grains and other food from a network of organic suppliers that it helped to establish.

A study undertaken in cooperation with the University of Kassel confirmed that Sieben Linden has enjoyed significant success in creating a low-impact settlement. It found that CO_2 emissions in the community were, per capita, around twenty-eight per cent of the German average—and just ten and six per cent, respectively, in heating and housing.

The community has grown rapidly over the last six years from thirty to around 100 members. It is divided into several neighbourhoods—to facilitate ease of decision-making and group-bonding—each of between fifteen and thirty people. These often develop around specific interests or themes. One of these is called Club 99 and is focused on developing a radically alternative, low-impact settlement model. Club 99 built the straw bale house by hand, is almost entirely self-reliant in food (it is vegan) and works the land by hand and horse. It also has a shared economy, with all income generated by the members pooled and allocated between them according to need.

The original goals that centred on self-sufficiency have been broadened to encompass the social and spiritual aspects of building and caring for a sustainable human settlement. More emphasis is now given to ensuring that the community is accessible to and replicable by more mainstream people and there are plans to significantly increase the number of training programmes offered. Here, the federated nature of the community is seen as a great strength, so that Club 99, for example, can continue to explore means of radically reducing its ecological footprint while other neighbourhoods focus on other and more easily replicable models. The concept of 'Unity in Diversity' is seen as an important feature of the community experiment.

Ecovillage at Ithaca (EVI), United States

Central to the concerns of the designers of Ecovillage at Ithaca from the outset was ease of replication by middle-class Americans: "The ultimate goal of EVI is nothing less than to redesign the human habitat. We are creating a model community of some 500 people that will exemplify sustainable systems of living—systems that are not only practical in themselves but replicable by others." (EVI Mission Statement)

The vision for EVI was born during a coast-to-coast walk across the United States called 'The Global Walk for a Liveable World'. Several of those involved in leading the walk set in motion, on their return, the process that would result in the creation of one of North America's most high-profile ecovillages. The initial visioning meetings in 1991 involved around 100 people, out of which committees were created to explore such issues as creating a mission statement, looking for land to buy, legal issues and fundraising.

Over the course of the next year, a piece of land was identified (a semi-rural location less than two miles from Ithaca city in New York state, one of whose attractions was that car use would not be a prerequisite), EVI was registered as a non-profit association, the 175-acre site was purchased through loans from supporters, and the size of the active group fell to 50 members. The group decided to create the new settlement along cohousing lines, with the process of design and development of the ecovillage to be centrally managed.

In 1996, after four-and-a-half years of planning, designing and building, the first community members moved into FRoG (First Residents Group). By 2003, the Second Neighbourhood Group (SoNG) had been completed and the community population reached its current size of 160 (60 households). Design features include dense clustering to reduce footprint size, shared boiler systems, passive solar design, super-insulated walls, and duplex construction. Almost half of SoNG homes have photovoltaic panels, and some have solar hot-water heaters. FRoG uses forty per cent less gas and electricity than similar homes in the area and SoNG promises to be even more efficient.

Car-pooling and the use of public transport and bicycles are fairly common in the community, while the high levels of on-site employment (it is estimated that about sixty per cent of EVI's wage-earning adults work at least part-time within the ecovillage) significantly reduce the need for commuting. There are many hybrid electric vehicles and one car that runs on vegetable oil. Some households have dry composting toilets and those that do not use low-water flushing systems. One resident couple runs an on-site community-supported agriculture (CSA) organic farm that produces vegetables for the local farmers' market and a vegetable box scheme that together feed 1,000 people a week during the growing season. An organic berry farm CSA will start later in 2006. Some ninety per cent of EVI's land is left as open space for organic agriculture, woods, meadows and wetland.

EVI is a major player in an initiative to make Tompkins County, where it is located, more sustainable. Committees associated with this scheme are working on a city car-share scheme, a green development in the city, waste-management, sustainability circles in the schools and many other initiatives.

Consistent with its core educational objective, EVI places a strong emphasis on communicating its experience to the wider world. EVI was formed under the auspices of the Center for Religion, Ethics and Social Policy (CRESP) at Cornell University and has, since its inception, been an important resource for interns and research students at Cornell and a dozen other colleges and universities around North America: six masters students and two doctoral students have completed their theses on some aspect of life at EVI. In 2002, EVI developed a joint partnership with the Environmental Studies Department of Ithaca College. This partnership earned a $149,000 matching grant from the National Science Foundation to develop a curriculum on the 'Science of Sustainability'. This partnership has been highly fruit-ful, leading Ithaca College to make a commitment to become "one of the pre-mier college campuses in the country, modelling sustainability in all its aspects" according to the Provost.

EVI has also developed a high profile in the media: it has enjoyed sub-stantial national coverage, including features in the New York Times, CNN, PBS and National Public Radio. It has also had a fair amount of international media coverage.

Ecoovila, Brazil

Ecoovila is a small ecovillage in the heart of the Brazilian city of Porto Alegre whose core aim is to develop and demonstrate affordable, socially inclusive and eco-friendly building methods for the urban context. The core group behind the creation of the ecovillage was made up of eight professional fam-ilies dissatisfied with the negative social and ecological impacts of the dom-inant architectural ethic in Brazil. They were inspired by permaculture (a design system which is based on the study and imitation of natural systems) and were keen to see how these design principles could be applied to urban housing in ways that could be widely replicable.

In 2001, the group pooled their savings to buy a plot of 2.6 hectares and set about designing a settlement for twenty-eight families along permacul-ture lines. Predictably, they soon ran up against the city authorities, which had little or no previous exposure to many of the design features they wished to include. There followed a period of negotiation and awareness-raising before agreement was reached on the design of the new neighbourhood.

By late 2002, the group was ready to begin building. The full complement of twenty-eight families was signed up for the project and they decided to build individually to a more or less standard design as each family succeeded in raising the finance to do so. Today, twenty of the houses have been built, and construction on the remaining eight will begin soon.

All of the houses are oriented towards the sun, thus benefiting from pas-sive solar gain. A central fireplace is designed to maximise thermal mass (capacity to absorb heat during the middle of the day, which is radiated out during the colder evenings and nights). Hot water is provided by solar pan-els, and while there is a stand-by gas heating system, this is rarely required. Unusually for houses in Porto Alegre, the ecovillage dwellings have no air-conditioning. They are cooled by air-flow through an innovative system of subterranean chambers and above-ground galleries that are also used for

La Caravana del Arcoiris por la Paz celebrates its recent alliance with the Brazilian Ministry of Culture.

Above: Working with horses at Sieben Linden, Germany.
Below: Kids To The Country programme, The Farm ecovillage, Tennessee, USA.

Photovoltaic panels at the Centre for Alternative Technology in Wales.

Above: Ecovillage consultant and educator Max Lindegger at work. Below: Growing basil, Damanhur ecovillage, Italy.

Restoring degraded ecosystems, Trees for Life, Findhorn ecovillage, Scotland.

Ecovillage solidarity at ZEGG ecovillage, Germany.

Creating a mural at Kitezh ecovillage, Russia.

Clockwise from bottom left: Wind and solar power at Auroville, India; Launch of the Eko community currency, Findhorn ecovillage, Scotland; Replanting mangroves at Mbam ecovillage, Senegal; Ecodyfi's community-owned wind turbine, Wales; Workshop on building with natural materials for Bedouin villagers at Kibbutz Lotan, Israel.

growing herbs, spices and vines. Grass roofs—the first of their kind in Brazil—are used, both for aesthetic appeal and to help with cooling in the hot months of summer.

A high percentage of local materials is used, including bamboo, cob and clay bricks. All of the wood used in the buildings is locally sourced from certified sustainable suppliers. The sewage is treated in a biological, reed-bed water-treatment system, with the water coming out at the end of the process used to irrigate vegetables and flowers grown in the community's gardens.

A core aspiration of the ecovillage pioneers is to contribute, through the convivial and attractive nature of the design, to the emergence of a vibrant community. This is already happening and community members work together in gardening, hosting visitors interested in the project and a range of other activities.

There has been considerable interest in the project both from the media and among the general populace and increasingly, it is seen as being a community- and eco-friendly model for new settlements. The community throws open its doors to visitors every Saturday. A consultancy company has formed in the ecovillage, staffed by twelve of the residents and a further thirty associates, and is now working on a range of other projects inspired by Ecoovila. These include a second ecovillage very much along the lines of Ecoovila, on a nine-hectare site bought by fifty-six families. Plans are also at an early stage to build a third ecovillage settlement for sixty teachers and their families next to a school.

In addition, the consultancy company is designing landscaped gardens for a number of businesses in Porto Alegre. In several cases, these include environmental education centres for the workers and the wider public.

These five examples reveal something of the diversity within the ecovillage family. There are several strong contrasts here. The most obvious is between the new intentional communities of the US and Europe and the existing villages of Africa. (Auroville sits astride this contrast, sharing features with both.) Meanwhile, Sieben Linden has made as few concessions as it can in seeking to achieve the lowest possible ecological footprint, while the goal of both EVI and Ecoovila is to create a model that will be attractive to and replicable by mainstream, middle-class people, thus making some compromises in terms of the 'purity' of the experiment.

There are also sharp differences in scale and location. While Auroville is a small town, EVI and Sieben Linden are barely large enough to qualify as villages, while Ecoovila is a small urban neighbourhood. Five of the case studies are new-builds, whereas one (the Senegalese ecovillages) comprises pre-existing communities. In short, contrasts abound.

Given the great heterogeneity on display here, it is legitimate to question whether the very concept of ecovillages retains any true coherence; when the term is being used to describe such a variety of circumstance, vision and strategy, is it capable of retaining any real meaning? I believe that it can, based on five fundamental attributes that, to greater or lesser extents, all can be seen to share.

The first is the primacy of *community*. The ecovillage is, perhaps above all else, a response to the alienation and solitude of the modern condition. It responds to a hunger in people for a reconnection with others in meaningful community; for being useful and valued members of human-scale societies. The communitarian impulse has a slightly different flavour in indigenous, poor-country contexts such as Senegal, representing above all else the desire to preserve the more congenial dimensions of traditional values and ways of life that are coming under such onslaught from the forces of modernity.

Nor are the benefits of communalism limited to the conviviality of living in human-scale settlements. The sharing of resources and facilities that it permits also affords the opportunity for substantial savings in resource use. Communities that eat together and that share cars, garden tools and common heating systems are not only happier; they also tread more lightly on the Earth.

Second, ecovillages are *citizens' initiatives*, more or less entirely reliant, at least initially, on the resources, imagination and vision of community members themselves. In the main, this results from a widespread dissatisfaction with, even alienation from, government and other official bodies. Specifically, the co-opting of states, North and South, by corporate interests and their unwillingness or inability to engage seriously with growing problems of ecological dislocation and poverty has encouraged many citizens to find ways of working outside the system. This tends to give ecovillages a highly libertarian (perhaps 'liberated' is the better word) flavour, consequent on their having consciously stepped outside of the dominant social arrangements in order to create ways of working together that better meet their own needs.

True, both Auroville and the Senegalese ecovillages enjoy official donor support. Nonetheless, in both cases the ecovillage initiatives were generated by the communities themselves and remain palpably self-directed.

A third defining characteristic of all ecovillages is that they are in the business of *wresting back control over their own resources* and, ultimately, their own destinies. In the countries of the South, the battle-lines for control over resources between communities and corporations are very evident. Water is diverted away from small-scale farms to feed monoculture plantations and golf courses. Traditional fishermen watch powerless while factory ships suck up their catch. Tourist hotels throw out their pollution of sex abuse and prostitution while undermining cultural vitality and self-confidence.

The same drama also plays out, though less obviously to many, in the countries of the North. Local economies are flattened by out-of-town supermarkets, leaving consumers with little choice but to buy products that demean workers and degrade ecosystems around the world. Communities become dependent for the provision of employment on large and distant corporations for whose favours they need to compete by relaxing their labour and environmental regulations. Culture becomes commodified, standardised and dumbed down to a lowest common denominator.

Opposition to economic globalisation, then, provides a rallying point for ecovillagers around the world, an attempt to win back some measure of community control over the various dimensions of human life: how we grow our food, build our houses, generate our energy, create our livelihoods, entertain ourselves and each other.

The fourth characteristic common to all ecovillages is that at their heart lies a *strong body of shared values*—that some ecovillages refer to in terms of 'spirituality'. This is a somewhat controversial assertion, for there are many both within and without the ecovillage family who are suspicious of the term. Certainly, a good number of more mainstream ecovillages make no specific reference to spirituality, preferring to use terms such as 'free thinking', 'tolerant towards diverse beliefs', or suchlike. However, even beyond the explicitly spiritual communities such as Auroville, there is across the board within the ecovillage family a shared commitment to global justice, ecological restoration, rebuilding community, service to others (each community may use a different form of words) that amounts to more or less the same thing.

To quote from Bill Metcalf, the scholar of intentional communities: "While Kommune Niederkufungen [a German ecovillage, of which more in the next chapter] claims to be non-spiritual, it is obvious to me that their humanist, socialist and ecological aims have an almost spiritual dimension.

Members believe they have a mission to promote communal living, to be a model of cooperation, equality, equity and productivity; and to do what they can to promote world peace and ecological sustainability."

The final common characteristic, closely linked to the fourth, is that ecovillages act as *centres of research, demonstration and (in most cases) training*, each in their own specific field of exploration and expertise; be it in mangrove restoration, appropriate technology, sustainability education, low-impact living or whatever. That is, a core function of ecovillages is to develop new ideas, technologies and models that it then shares with the wider world. Even in pre-existing traditional villages such as Mbam and Faoune, at the heart of the ecovillage impulse within them is the drive to develop and share effective ways of addressing society-wide problems.

This is important for the sake of clarity in distinguishing ecovillages from the myriad initiatives in rural and urban eco-regeneration that are primarily to do with improving conditions locally. Ecovillages are always in service of a wider goal.

This analysis, then, offers a new definition of ecovillages as:

> *Private citizens' initiatives in which the communitarian impulse is of central importance, that are seeking to win back some measure of control over community resources, that have a strong shared values base (often referred to as 'spirituality') and that act as centres of research, demonstration and (in most cases) training.*

This, then, provides an introductory glimpse into the world of ecovillages. The next chapter will examine thematically some of the key areas in which ecovillages have sought to create meaningful, alternative models on the path to a more convivial and sustainable world.

Chapter 3

Saying Yes:
beyond the politics of protest

'*One No: Many Yeses*'—title of recent book by Paul Kingsnorth

While world leaders gathered at the G8 summit in Gleneagles, Scotland in July 2005, about forty miles down the road in Stirling, another parallel gathering was taking place. Several thousand activists created a temporary ecovillage to model a practical alternative to what they saw as the wasteful policies being promoted in Gleneagles. A small but significant contingent of around forty of those building the ecovillage were themselves more permanent ecovillagers, residents in the Findhorn Foundation community near Inverness.

Nine compost toilets and more than twenty greywater systems were built in just a few days. These were maintained throughout the week, with the waste product disposed of in non-polluting ways. Power for lighting was provided by wind turbines and solar panels. Thirteen kitchens were set up and the kitchen waste composted and left as a resource for the local community allotment. The kitchens served largely fair trade and/or organic food, much of it produced locally.

In the words of the US activist Starhawk, who was part of the core organising team: "We created a camp that helped foster the social relations of shared power and responsibility. There were many moments where the camp set-up embodied anarchism at its best—everyone working like a happy, humming beehive with coordination but without coercion, people eager to take on tasks, joyfully doing hard physical work because it needed to be done, building, carrying, designing and creating and having a really good time together."

The BBC's news website carried a report on its front page under the headline "Ecovillage is model for us all". It quoted local officials as saying: "They want to leave the site as they found it," and "They're making a good point. We're very supportive of what they're doing (recycling greywater) and it's something we'd like to encourage."

The Stirling action can trace very specific roots back to the German peaceniks in the 1970s and 1980s who built 'ökodorf' next to the military bases where they camped and against which they were protesting. These, too, attempted to model ways of living that tread more gently on the Earth. The temporary ecovillage at Stirling illustrates the primary gift of ecovillages to the wider sustainability family; namely, the impulse to move beyond protest and to create models of more sane, just and sustainable ways of living.

In this chapter, we will explore some of the models that have been developed by ecovillages around the world in numerous fields of activity:

- the design of low-impact human settlements
- promoting sustainable local economies
- organic, locally based food production and processing
- Earth restoration
- revival of participatory, community-scale governance
- social inclusion
- peace activism and international solidarity, and
- holistic, whole person education.

This is not an exhaustive list of the areas in which ecovillages are engaged: many others could be added, including water management, healing, culture and arts, waste management and recycling, spiritual enquiry and so on. The reference section at the end of this book points the reader in the direction of more detailed books, websites and other resources. The aim here is to focus on some of the most notable areas where successes have been recorded.

The design of low-impact human settlements

At the very heart of the rationale for creating ecovillages is the desire to construct human settlements that tread less heavily on the Earth and in which people are more healthily and sustainably integrated into the non-human world.

Two broad, though complementary—and, to some degree, over-lapping—approaches can be discerned in the ways that various ecovillages have sought to create low-impact settlements. The first can be described as the 'low-tech' approach, as exemplified by Sieben Linden, where a conscious attempt is made to reduce the use of fossil fuels, to simplify design and reduce needs and costs, and to make as much use as possible of locally available and recycled materials. The second can be described as high-tech and involves the use of state-of-the-art ecological technologies, even though these are often more expensive in investment costs than conventional alternatives.

A number of communities in the UK have pioneered low-tech models. Of these, the most celebrated is Tinkers' Bubble, forty acres of woodland, orchards and pasture in Somerset that is home to a small community of twelve adults and four children. They have strict rules banning the use of fossil fuels (with the exception of transport—the residents share two cars—and the paraffin they use in their lamps).

Shelters are either small, canvas dwellings or other temporary structures or, increasingly, beautiful houses made from wood—cut in their own forest, using hand-saws—and straw bales, wattle and daub and thatch. They heat their homes with wood, cut their hay with scythes and milk the cows, weed the fields and harvest the crops by hand. In addition, they have set up a small windmill and some solar panels, built compost toilets and bought a wood-powered steam engine for milling timber. The community is partly self-sufficient in organic food, with the remaining grains and nuts coming from a bulk organic distributor.

In the words of commentator George Monbiot: "They haven't yet solved all their problems, but they have shown that a life which requires scarcely any fossil fuel consumption is still possible. . . . One hundred and fifty years after he published *Walden*, Henry David Thoreau is alive and well in Somerset."

Tinkers' Bubble has set an important precedent in Britain by winning permission, after a legal struggle that went to the Court of Appeals, for people to live in a low-impact manner on their own land. Community resident Simon Fairlie has also been the driving force behind the creation of Chapter 7, an influential organisation seeking to reform rural planning regulations in such a way that it becomes easier to replicate what has been achieved at Tinkers' Bubble.

Another low-impact UK ecovillage that has had legal struggles is Brithdir Mawr in Pembrokeshire, west Wales. This community comprises ten adults and five children and is based on principles of 'simplicity, sustainability and spirit'. Electrical power is generated on-site by solar panels, a micro-hydro unit and a wind generator. The land is worked by three farm horses and the community is largely self-reliant in vegetables.

A core objective of the community is to demonstrate that it is possible to make a living from the products growing on their own land. This has led to the development of a wide range of traditional crafts, including basketry, rustic gate making, woodturning, spinning, weaving and felt making. The community is also engaged in much food-processing, including the bottling and pickling of vegetables and the production of fruit wines.

A number of the buildings in the community are largely built from local materials and it is one of these, the Roundhouse, which has been the cause of the community's involvement in the legal process over the last several years. This is a very low-impact dwelling, self-built by community residents Jane Faith and Tony Wrench, which has a round wood frame of hand-cut Douglas fir forest thinning. The walls are cob wood with recycled double-glazed windows and there is a straw-insulated turf roof. Heating is provided by wood stove, electricity is solar-generated, and water is piped from a neighbouring mountain. The house has a compost toilet and grey water is diverted through a reed bed. No cement was used or building waste produced in the construction and the structure cost a total of £3,000. The house was to have been demolished over Easter 2004, but won a late reprieve and its legality will next be considered in July 2006.

The second ecovillage strategy for reducing ecological footprints is based less on values of radical simplification than on the adoption of state-of-the-art, highly energy-efficient technologies. Here, ecovillages often play the role of innovators, able by dint of their small scale and strong, shared value base to move more quickly than conventional communities. Many ecovillages have some combination of the following devices: solar water-heaters, photovoltaic generators, combined heat-and power district energy systems, geothermal energy generation, highly energy-efficient and non-toxic building techniques, biological waste-water treatment systems, hybrid electric vehicles and so on.

Just a few of the many examples of best practice within the ecovillage family will be given here. The Damanhur community in Italy has invested heavily in advanced technologies. Heating stoves have been introduced that use a sophisticated system that regulates combustion and recycles ninety per cent of the heat produced for other functions. Supported by regional and European subsidies, the community has installed twenty photovoltaic electric generators that produce enough electricity to meet the domestic needs of approximately 130 people. Around thirty solar water heaters, together with a number of small hydroelectric and wind turbines, are also in use. Energy-generating technologies using both methane and hydrogen have been introduced, along with electronically controlled stoves for burning wood chip briquettes.

Damanhur's houses are highly insulated, cutting the need for heating to twenty-five per cent of the average Italian home. The community is also switching to low-impact vehicles: electric cars for short journeys and methane gas and LPG for longer-distance trips. A biodiesel pump located in the main car park has reduced the community's consumption of diesel fuel by 3,000 litres per month.

In a similar vein, the Sólheimar community in Iceland has introduced innovative technologies that have permitted it to reduce its ecological impact significantly while becoming self-sufficient in energy and food. A number of eco-friendly buildings have been built over the last fifteen years, the most impressive of which is Sesselja House, an 'Eco-centre' that hosts conferences, meetings and educational courses. It employs energy-efficient lighting, earth-chilled and geothermally warmed air circulation and heat recovery, solar photovoltaic and geothermal electricity, and several additional innovative features not previously known in Iceland. It is the first contemporary building in Iceland that is PVC-free. In addition, it has the first solid/liquid separation system of its kind in Iceland, which converts solid sewage into soil.

Sesselja House also incorporates a number of simpler technologies that serve to further reduce its ecological impact, including the use of recycled tyre rubber for floors, sustainably harvested timber products for trusses and the substitution of rammed earth for cement. The paint used is made from organic oils, the walls are insulated with Icelandic lambs' wool, and the roof is insulated using recycled paper. The community has a hot spring that generates near boiling water at twelve to fifteen gallons per second. This is more than adequate to provide central heating for all buildings, hot water, a warm swimming pool with hot tub, and supplies for a large number of greenhouses that grow vegetables and nursery trees year-round. The community was the first institution in Iceland to practise organic food production.

The Camphill family of communities, to which Sólheimar is related though not formally a member (both draw their inspiration from the teachings of Rudolf Steiner and are dedicated to integrating special needs and non-special needs people into vibrant, convivial communities), also tends to lay a strong emphasis on the use of efficient ecological design. Five neighbouring Camphill communities in County Kilkenny in Ireland, for example, can be seen as an eco-cluster. Four use wood chip and wood pellet systems to meet their heating requirements, and a wood chip production and distribution company is being set up to supply the communities and a network of renewable energy users that has developed in the area.

One of the Camphill communities is heated by a biogas plant—the first of its kind in Ireland—that processes 5,000 tonnes of food waste annually, converting it into biogas and organic fertiliser that supplies local farms. The communities also use solar water-heaters and are in the process of creating a biodiesel production and distribution plant to fuel the community vehicles. One of the communities has a car-pool of seven vehicles for a resident population of eighty people. All buildings are designed to high ecological standards and a building company has been set up to develop and disseminate their expertise in this field.

Lebensgarten ecovillage in Germany has also played an important pioneering role in the introduction of new eco-technologies. It was the first community in its region to introduce photovoltaic generators, a combined heat and power generator, solar-powered cars and solar warm water-heaters. These technologies are now widely used throughout Germany, with the Lebensgarten-based shop, ÖkoLoggia, playing an important role in popularising them locally. Lebensgarten now has seven photovoltaic systems, eight thermal heating systems and two solar-powered cars. Its car-pool of five cars is used by fifteen people.

Nor are efforts in the field of technological innovation limited to the countries of the North. Both Auroville and GEN Senegal have been active in the dissemination of solar technologies to villages off the grid. Working closely with the Ladakh Ecological Development Group (LEDeG)—an indigenous NGO it founded in 1978—the Ladakh Project (a founder member of GEN) has introduced a number of solar technologies into the mountainous kingdom in northern India. These include photovoltaic power for lighting, solar water heaters and cookers, and solar room-heating systems to combat the freezing winters. The Project has also been active in introducing hydraulic ram pumps for lifting irrigation and drinking water, and micro-hydro installations and small wind turbines for electricity production. The work of the Project has helped to generate something of a renewable energy revolution in Ladakh, with many of the technologies being taken up on a large scale by government and other voluntary agencies.

A striking feature of most ecovillages—low- and high-tech alike—that enables them to significantly reduce their ecological footprints is their more or less holistic and integrated character, enabling them to increase internal resource flows and reduce the need for external inputs. For example, kitchen wastes can easily be made available as compost for the community gardens, coppicing from community woodlands feeds the residents' stoves and the wood-pellet heating systems, biologically treated waste water is diverted to the food-producing areas, and harvested and scrap wood gets used in new building projects. Moreover, since most ecovillages provide considerable employment on-site, there tends to be a significantly reduced need for transport. These benefits are partly a function of intentional design, partly a function of scale: it is simply easier for resource flows to be integrated and waste reduced in communities at the ecovillage scale.

What makes ecovillages especially effective as catalysts for change is that the primary object of activities such as those listed above is less to do with making life comfortable for ecovillage residents than demonstrating the viability of new, more ecologically benign approaches that they then promote and disseminate. In many cases, this happens naturally as a result of visits by local people. In the area around the cluster of Camphill communities in south-east Ireland, for example, wood pellet heating systems have now been introduced by three kindergartens and an integrated arts college and learning centre. Such is the level of interest in the biogas technology that has been introduced that one of the Camphill communities is in the process of establishing an independent biogas design, build and operate company—once again, the first in Ireland.

Many ecovillages also run training in the building methods and other technologies they have developed. A number also have consultancy services. Ecological Solutions based at the Crystal Waters ecovillage in Queensland, Australia, provides technical services to resource-management and sustainability-related initiatives across Australia, New Zealand and Asia, specialising in the design of low-impact building and settlements.

The consultancy service at the Centre for Alternative Technology (CAT) in Wales, meanwhile, provides expertise to government, businesses, educational bodies and non-profit organisations in a wide range of technical areas: renewable energy; energy conservation; environmental building; organic

FINDHORN FOUNDATION FOOTPRINT ANALYSIS

The benefits deriving from a combination of low-impact and eco-efficient technologies and integrated resource flows are well illustrated by an ecological footprint study undertaken of the Findhorn Foundation ecovillage in Scotland. The community numbers around 400 people, much of whose food is provided by a community-supported organic agriculture scheme. It is a net exporter of renewable energy (wind and solar) and is making a long-term transition from caravans to highly energy-efficient dwellings.

Sewage is treated in a Living Machine biological waste-water treatment system. The community has its own bank and currency and employs most of its members on site, thus reducing the need for commuting. Along with Crystal Waters in Australia and Lebensgarten in Germany, Findhorn has been awarded a UN Habitat Best Practice citation.

An ecological footprint study was undertaken of the community in 2005. (Ecological footprinting is a tool for measuring a given population's resource use, measured in the common denominator of hectares of productive land.)

The study found that the per capita footprint of the average Findhorn community member is 3.25 hectares. This represents sixty per cent of the national UK average, meaning that residents at Findhorn use forty per cent fewer resources than the national average. While this can be considered impressive, it remains true that if everyone in the world enjoyed a standard of living similar to that of a Findhorn ecovillager, we would still need 1.8 planet Earths to provide for our needs (compared to three planet Earths for the UK as a whole).

The community scores especially well in the area of food, a significant proportion of which is local and organic and prepared communally, with a footprint just thirty-seven per cent of the national average. The benefits of shared facilities and a spirit of voluntary simplicity are also strongly in evidence in a footprint only forty-seven per cent of the national average associated with the ownership of household and personal goods.

Findhorn's footprint is almost identical to that of BedZED, the London developer-led eco-settlement (3.25 compared to 3.20 hectares per capita). However, BedZED's footprint relating specifically to the building and heating of homes is less than half that of Findhorn. This is partly due to the continued use of energy-inefficient caravans for some members' accommodation. It also suggests that Findhorn, in common with many other ecovillages, could achiever significant improvements through the adoption of more coherent, settlement-wide eco-design features including, for example, wood-chip district heating systems and heat-sharing between dwellings.

waste and sewage systems; water supply, treatment and conservation; ecological landscaping; and setting up and running green visitor facilities.

The Ecovillage Institute (EVI), based in Findhorn, exports techniques and
models developed within the ecovillage. EVI is working in environments as
diverse as Bolivia, Ethiopia and Harlow New Town in Hertfordshire.
Findhorn introduced the first Living Machine—a highly efficient, biological
sewage-treatment system—in the UK. This is now widely disseminated
through the country and the Findhorn-based engineering company Living
Technologies has provided technical assistance to a number of other projects, including BedZED, the Earth Centre and the Body Shop.

Building and technology enterprises serve as another way in which ecovillages disseminate their low-impact methods into the wider community.
Many ecovillage companies have 'learned by doing' the art of building beautiful, energy-efficient structures, often with a high local material content.
These then become resources for their entire regions. The German ecovillage Lebensgarten—which, interestingly, has transformed one of Hitler's
munitions factories, once staffed with Polish and Russian slave labour, into
a centre of sustainability and inspiration—has both active construction
companies and a specialist shop—ÖkoLoggia—which sells building materials to which ecologically sensitive builders travel from far and wide.

There is a strong tradition of ecovillage-based renewable energy enterprises. We have already seen the scale and range of energy technologies disseminated by enterprises in Auroville. AES Engineering at Findhorn remains
the only solar panel manufacturer in Scotland, while Dulas Engineering in
Machynlleth, created by a team of former CAT employees, manufactures
and installs all sorts of renewable technologies—including solar, biogas and
micro-hydro—both in the UK and in numerous countries of the South.

Promoting sustainable local economies

The process of economic globalisation has severely undercut the viability
of local economies. Corporate subsidies and unfair trade arrangements
have created a global economy in which huge volumes of produce are
shipped hither and thither across the world. This delivers profits to the corporations that control production and distribution, while undermining
communities, local economies and ecosystems alike.

So all-pervasive is this global system that people feel increasingly powerless to oppose it. While the fair trade movement has made important

strides, it constitutes a minuscule fraction of total global trade, and in most product areas, consumers find it ever more difficult to find affordable locally and/or ethically produced goods.

The ecovillage response to this thorny problem takes three forms. First, there is a strong impulse towards 'voluntary simplicity', the conscious decision to live more simply. This takes its purest form in communities such as Tinkers' Bubble and Sieben Linden that are committed to modelling low-impact lifestyles, but pervades the ecovillage movement.

Thus ecovillages tend to be places where there is a significant sharing and recycling of clothes, toys and equipment of all kinds. The seventy-two members of the Kommune Niederkaufungen ecovillage in Germany share seven cars, two washing machines and two video recorders. Levels of television ownership in ecovillages tend to be especially low, both because of the cost of the equipment and licence and because of the medium's subversive role in promoting consumerism. The Ladakh Project even runs 'No TV' weeks, aimed at resisting the most damaging elements of non-Ladakhi culture. In the place of television, ecovillagers tend to turn to homegrown entertainment: choirs, concerts and theatre groups abound.

There is, in addition, a strong impulse to redefine the relationship to work, not as a chore but an act of service and enjoyment. Thus, the Twin Oaks ecovillage in Virginia declares: "We use a trust-based labor system in which all work is valued equally. Its purpose is to organise work and share it equitably, giving each member as much flexibility and choice as possible. Work is not seen as just a means to an end; we try to make it an enjoyable part of our lives." In Findhorn, work is described as 'love in action'.

Ecovillages are also involved in campaigns to promote the ethics of voluntary simplicity. A number act as nodal points for local groups of the Slow Food movement, an initiative whose aim is to "protect the pleasures of the table from the homogenisation of modern fast food and life". One of these, the Italian ecovillage Torri Superiori, is also an active participant in the emergence of Decroissance Soutenable (Sustainable Contraction), a movement that is growing fast in Italy and France, geared towards promoting lower consumption in order to achieve higher quality of life.

Second, there is within ecovillages a strong, though admittedly weakening, tradition of economic solidarity: that is, a broad sharing of resources with all income going into a common pot, and the collective taking some measure of responsibility for meeting members' needs. This permits the community to provide a wide range of shared services, to facilitate a redistribution of wealth within the collective and to help communities reduce their dependence on the global economy.

Perhaps the economy of solidarity finds its strongest expression in the Camphill communities. Their core economic principle is the following: "In a community of human beings working together, the well being of the community will be the greater, the less the individual claims for himself the proceeds of the work he has himself done; i.e. the more of these proceeds he makes over to his fellow workers, and the more his own requirements are satisfied, not out of his work, but out of the work done by others." This ensures that frugality and generosity are built into economic behaviour. The Norwegian Camphill family of communities redistributes some of its surplus through the 'East Fund', created to help the setting up of Camphill communities in Estonia, Latvia, Poland, Russia and the Czech Republic. Over the last fifteen years, around £1 million has been channelled through the fund and the Norwegian communities have sent builders to Russia to teach straw bale building techniques.

The economy of the Kommune Niederkaufungen ecovillage is strongly communitarian in nature. There is no private property other than clothes and personal effects. All the profits from each of the eleven work groups— carpentry, seminar centre, construction, kitchen, organic gardening, dairy farm, leatherwork, architecture services, kindergarten, metalwork and construction—go into the common purse. The community's businesses earn enough to meet communal living costs of around €50,000 per month. When members need money for personal matters, they simply take it from a box of cash that sits in the office. They do not ask anyone's approval, but record how it will be used. Expenditures are displayed at the end of each month according to how it was spent, but with no mention of who spent it. Bill Metcalf observes: "The system works remarkably well."

The Twin Oaks community in Virginia, US, also provides a living for all of its 100 members, including health insurance, from the profits it makes from its community-owned hammock, furniture and tofu making businesses. Some members of The Farm community in Tennessee, US, meanwhile, have developed an ingenious system, the Second Foundation, in which participants pool income that is used to provide low-interest loans to community businesses. The interest on these loans provides members with accounting and legal services, group medical and pension funds, while the capital continues to revolve in the form of low-interest loans among community initiatives.

This has parallels with a pensions scheme being developed among Camphill communities in Norway. Here, eighty participants have contributed about £500,000 into a pension fund that is secured by the Camphill Village Trust of Norway, conservatively estimated at a value of £9 million. These funds provide loans to the Norwegian Camphill Trust (this cannot exceed twenty per cent of the total invested), loans to individual Camphill members and equity investments in ethical banks. The interest payments on the loans pay pension dividends while the capital circulates in support of life-enhancing projects.

A third type of economic innovation explored by ecovillages is experimentation with community currencies and banks. Two of the most successful such initiatives are in Damanhur in Italy and the Findhorn Foundation community in Scotland. Both have set up their own banks to mobilise their members' savings for community initiatives and their own currencies to keep money circulating locally (rather than quickly leaving the area as tends to happen with national and supra-national currencies).

Within Damanhur, the role of banker is taken on by the community's real estate cooperative. This body was created as a vehicle for investing the savings of community members in the purchase of land and the building of accommodation, workshop and office space for community members and businesses. It has also come to play a role more akin to that of a mainstream bank, helping to identify business opportunities and providing loans and advice to community members. At the end of every year, the real estate cooperative undertakes a study of the community economy, identifying which goods and services still need to be bought in from the outside and seeking to promote new community enterprises to fill these gaps.

The Findhorn Foundation community has created Ekopia, a body with the status of an industrial provident society, to recycle locally the savings of its members. Projects in need of investment are identified and share issues are raised against them. Each investor has one voting share only, irrespective of how much they invest, thus promoting a strongly cooperative ethic. This has enabled the community to draw on the financial resources of both current members and the wider Findhorn family, many of whom were previous members and all of whom share the community's vision to create a more self-reliant and low-impact human settlement.

The first of the share issues raised by Ekopia involved 250 individuals investing a total of £225,000 in a community-led buy-out of the community store, the Phoenix shop. Share issues have also been raised to provide finance to the Findhorn Foundation (£100,000 has been raised) and the community educational facility, NewBold House (£25,000). Further share issues to finance the purchase of new windmills and affordable, eco-friendly houses are in the pipeline.

This system delivers multiple benefits to the community. Investors become co-owners of the businesses in which they buy shares, gain a five per cent discount on all purchases in the Phoenix shop and a dividend reflecting the growth in the value of the business. Ekopia calculates that together, these various benefits equal a return on an investment of one £500 share of up to £100 per annum, compared to around £15 of interest payments on £500 deposited in the bank. In addition, ecovillage businesses are able to draw on the monetary savings of community members without needing to pay commercial bank fees and interest rates. Community businesses make a saving of up to £2,000 per annum on bank fees.

The community currencies—the Credito in Damanhur and the Eko in Findhorn—both trade at parity with the national currency. While all transactions within Damanhur are undertaken using Creditos, residents and visitors to Findhorn have a choice and most use both national and community currencies. In both places, all goods and services can be bought with the community currency.

It is estimated that the first issue of 18,000 Ekos in Findhorn generated a turnover of £150,000 in the first year of the scheme, almost more than eight full spending cycles. This is money that has stuck around, shaken plenty of hands and provided much valuable lubrication to the community economy. For sure, many of the products for sale within the community shop and other businesses originate outside the community and so money will necessarily continue to leave the system to pay for them. Nonetheless, the use of Creditos and Ekos has prevented a substantial leakage of purchasing power, making it easier for local enterprises to emerge.

In summary, the creation of Ekopia and of the Ekos in the Findhorn Foundation community and of the real estate company and the Credito in Damanhur have gone some way towards setting up a virtuous circle in which everyone wins. Investors gain more in terms of both financial returns and ownership of community businesses. Businesses get access to credit at a cheaper rate than through the conventional banking system. Expanding local businesses generate extra employment and purchasing power. And more of that purchasing power remains within the community. This is a manifestation of what American commentator Michael Shuman describes as "the synergies that emerge when local investment is combined with local ownership, local production and local employment".

Less easy to measure is the strong social dividend inherent in the feelings of ownership and participation felt by members of the community towards their own economy. Decisions relating to consumption, investment and work cease to be made purely according to criteria of profit maximisation. The divorce between head and heart that the current global economy enforces (whereby people often make consumer choices that they know to be socially or ecologically exploitative because they feel they have little choice) is, to some degree at least, overcome. This ecovillage model enables people to bring back into alignment their desire for justice and sustainability with their aspiration to live well and happily. An important split in the soul of modern man begins to be healed.

Together, these various economic strategies—voluntary simplicity, economic solidarity and the use of community banks and currencies—have helped many ecovillage economies attain a distinctive and uncommon level of vitality. One sees bakeries, theatres, shops and cafés that draw in visitors from far and wide. Local organic cheeses, wines, fruit and vegetables combine great quality with very low food miles. Crafts studios turn out beautiful ceramics, textiles, carvings and candles. Schools and training centres for both children and adults flourish. Publishing houses, printing presses, solar panels manufacturers, waste-water system designers, consulting companies . . . . Everywhere there is evidence of economic vitality and diversification.

A study in 2002 by the local enterprise company into the economic impact of the Findhorn Foundation calculated that the community generates 400 jobs and over £5 million of business annually in northern Scotland. It commented on the value to the Scottish economy of the community's diversification into activities beyond its original educational heartland. Meanwhile, Damanhur's economy goes from strength to strength, its latest expansion being the purchase of a former Olivetti factory located nearby, a metaphor perhaps for the evolution from a corporate to an ecovillage-based society.

Organic, locally based food production and processing

One sector in which ecovillages have tended to be especially active is food. The Danish ecovillage Svanholm, for example, was among the first organic producers in the country and the first large organic farm. The community runs a mixed farm of 570 acres that includes herds of 200 sheep and 100 cows, together with the production of vegetables, potatoes, grains and herbs. The community also pioneered the wholesaling of organic foods to cooperative supermarkets, a marketing technique imitated by numerous other growers and supermarkets in Denmark.

EarthShare at the Findhorn Foundation is the UK's first, and still largest, community-supported agriculture (CSA) scheme. The CSA is a model that enables farmers and consumers to share the risks and benefits associated with growing and marketing organic vegetables: in the case of EarthShare, around 200 subscribers receive a weekly box of produce with minimal associated packaging and transport in exchange for a subscription fee and some labour inputs. EarthShare has been used by the Soil Association, Britain's foremost promoter of organic agriculture, as a training and demonstration site for CSAs, of which there are now around twenty in the country.

The Earthaven ecovillage in North Carolina, US, has also developed substantial organic agricultural production by developing an innovative form of support to its members. Neither the community nor its members had the start-up capital required to establish farm-scale production. The community made available common land to be leased by individual community members at affordable rates and on condition that they use specified sustainable farming practices. Three other forms of subsidy are offered to members to enable them to move into agricultural production. First, the community reimburses the costs of sustainable logging and other operations to clear land for farming. Second, the costs of any permanent agricultural infrastructure such as storage sheds, barns, animal pens, fences, irrigation ponds, etc. are reimbursed. Finally, the community offers sweat-equity trades to certain incoming members who help clear land and build farming infrastructure.

Today, there are three different agricultural initiatives within the community: two using a grass-rotational pasturage system, and one a Biodynamic vegetable market gardening business. These have been able to emerge because the community agreed to share the investment costs and shoulder the risk alongside its members.

Among its numerous innovations in the field of agriculture, The Ladakh Project introduced the first solar greenhouses in Ladakh, enabling villagers to grow vegetables all year round. There are now thousands throughout the region. The Project also runs a campaign about the hazards of pesticides, fungicides and chemical fertilisers and a seed-saving programme to promote the cultivation and protection of local varieties of grains and legumes.

Earth restoration

Most current environmental campaigns are focused, rightly, on attempting to limit . . . destruction—preventing the extinction of whales, the rainforests from being destroyed etc. Those of us alive now will determine which of our fellow species and intact ecosystems survive into the future. However, even if all the ecological devastation were to stop tomorrow, we would still be left with a world whose life-carrying capacity has been substantially reduced. Thus, the damage-limitation campaigns need to be complemented with initiatives to increase the diversity and vitality of those parts of the world that have already been severely degraded. This is the new field of science and practice known as Ecological Restoration: how to help the Earth heal.

This statement, taken from the website of the ecological restoration charity Trees for Life, based at the Findhorn Foundation ecovillage, provides a clear illustration of the ecovillage impulse to move beyond the politics of protest. Of the great Caledonian Forest that once covered over 1.5 million hectares in the Highlands of Scotland, today just one per cent remains. Trees for Life was created in 1981 with the vision "to restore a wild forest, which is there for its own sake, as a home for wildlife and to fulfil the ecological functions necessary for the wellbeing of the land itself".

By 2005, more than half a million native trees had been planted and a further 150,000 naturally occurring seedlings had been protected with fencing from over-grazing by deer (the main factor preventing the forest from renewing itself), so that they can regenerate of their own accord. The whole fabric of the web of life in the forest is becoming successfully re-established and the ecosystem is being restored towards full health. More than 1,000 volunteers, from teenagers to 70-year-olds, have taken part in this forest restoration work, often with life-changing effects.

Trees for Life has won a number of prestigious awards, including the Millennium Marque Award given to projects which "demonstrate environmental excellence for the 21st century". The work of Trees for Life has also inspired the establishment of several other restoration projects, including Moor Trees, which works to restore native oak woodland on Dartmoor in England.

Similar Earth restoration initiatives abound in the ecovillage movement. We noted the efforts of Auroville in India in planting more than two million trees, and of Mbam ecovillage in restoring degraded mangroves on the Senegalese coastline. The Colombian ecovillage Gaviotas has planted 8,000 hectares of Caribbean pine trees in a savannah that had been unproductive for centuries and where it had been considered impossible to plant trees in such acidic soil. More than a decade later, this has resulted in an increase in precipitation of ten per cent, converting Las Gaviotas from an arid wasteland into a net supplier of drinking water.

Also in Colombia, the Sasardi Integrated Reserve and Ecovillage is a private conservation area dedicated to the preservation of the Choco bioregion, an area of outstanding biodiversity that is increasingly under threat from infrastructure development projects. A small group went to live in the area in 1985 and since then, the ecovillage has been the catalyst for a wide variety of activities aimed at protecting the cultural and ecological integrity of the region. Foremost among these has been a programme to protect the endangered leatherback sea turtle. More than 50,000 turtle hatchlings have been spawned in the hatcheries established by the ecovillage.

The ecovillage community has also initiated environmental education programmes in schools, along with projects to help people manufacture handicrafts from sustainably harvested local materials, to involve midwives and medicine men in research into medicinal plants and herbs, and the establishment of sustainable fish breeding and animal rearing.

The Farm in Tennessee has engaged in extensive restoration measures, such as riparian repairs and watershed protection, conservation set-asides (including around 1,000 acres of wildlife habitat, as a contribution to the establishment of the Big Swan Headwaters Preserve in 1997), forest reseeding, highland prairie management, wildlife identification and protection. Community members played a leading role in the creation of the Swan Conservation Trust, a non-profit organisation dedicated to the protection, preservation and restoration of wildlife habitat and water quality on the Western Highland Rim of Tennessee. This now protects more than 1,500 contiguous acres from logging, subdivision and development, and engages in tree-planting and other measures to slow the water run-off in this ecologically sensitive area.

Some $400,000 was raised in a community-initiated subscription at The Farm to buy the Highland Woods conservation area before paper companies could log it. The Farm-initiated organisation Save Our Water Now was created as a local grassroots effort to stop deep-well injection into the aquifer by pesticide and herbicide companies.

Sólheimar ecovillage is an important participant in Iceland's South-West Forestry reforestation programme. Every year, some 17,500 trees are planted on the Sólheimar estate. A target for the community's reforestation effort has been set at 450,000 trees.

In response to the disastrous complex of events that have devastated Portugal's indigenous forests—devastating fires, climate change, and a sharp decline in the number of cork oaks—Tamera ecovillage has planted 10,000 young trees which it has maintained through the drought that gripped the country over the last eighteen months.

Kibbutz Lotan's activities are rooted in 'Tikun Olam'—the Jewish concept for repairing and transforming the world. Its Center for Creative Ecology began with the creation of a small desert organic garden and has today expanded to include a unique desert ecological education centre, a migratory bird reserve and educational nature trails.

Revival of participatory, community-scale governance

Much attention tends to be placed on the technological features of ecovillages—the windmills, eco-friendly buildings and so on. Ecovillagers themselves lay at least as much emphasis on the social dimension: the challenge of finding satisfactory and inclusive forms of community governance and wellbeing. This is among the most challenging tasks faced by ecovillages and lies at the root of the collapse of not a few of them. Moreover, given the progressive breakdown in community structures, especially in the countries of the North, this appears to be a vital area of research if we are to see the rebirth of vibrant, self-governing communities.

There are three principal dimensions to ecovillage efforts in this field: promoting a culture of trust and compassion, creating effective decision-making procedures and working with conflict. Most ecovillages seek to establish a culture of trust among their members through more honest and transparent communication. This has been a priority for the German ecovillage ZEGG (whose name is the German acronym for the Center for Experimental Culture Design), at the heart of whose mission is an exploration of the foundations for a non-violent way of living.

Over the last twenty-five years, ZEGG has developed a community communication tool called 'Forum'. Part community meeting and part ensemble theatre performance, the Forum is a way for people to come together to re-discover the truth of each individual's experiences within the larger context of a shared collective vision. This tool has been exported to a number of other ecovillages where it is now used as a way of building trust, encouraging transparency of communication and exploring shared values and visions.

Decision-making in most ecovillages is made on the basis of consensus, or near-consensus principles. This means that decisions are not taken until unanimity or near unanimity has been reached. It is true that this can slow the process, sometimes for long periods, however the aim is to seek accommodation, to find ways of arriving at a synthesis of the best in divergent perspectives and to avoid the alienation of minorities, as happens all too frequently in more conventional decision-making structures.

The smaller the ecovillage, the greater are the chances that all members will be involved in the decision-making process and that pure consensus will be adhered to. As communities grow in size and complexity, however, this becomes more difficult, and most make the transition to some form of participatory democracy, with decisions taken even where a small minority continues to dissent. This trend can be seen in Sieben Linden and ZEGG, in both of which a growing number of decisions is taken within committees and small specialist working groups.

The International Institute for Facilitation and Consensus, that has its roots in the Mexican ecovillage of Huehuecoyotl, acts as a centre for research and training in the field of consensus decision-making and facilitation. Relying on a group of skilled facilitators around the world, a good number of whom are or have been based in ecovillages, the Institute takes participatory communication tools and techniques developed in ecovillages and other sister initiatives out into more mainstream contexts. Recent IIFAC projects have included the Women's Peace Village Project in Ecuador funded by US State Dept Bureau of Educational and Cultural Affairs, and the Regional Forum for Reflection on the Millennium Goals in Mexico.

The final strand of ecovillage efforts in the field of reviving community-level governance is that of conflict facilitation. All too often, communities—both intentional and conventional—are dogged by destructive conflicts. Ecovillages aim not to suppress conflict but rather to harness its power creatively, encouraging the expression of uncomfortable emotions in non-destructive ways. Towards this end, many ecovillages have developed formal conflict mediation structures and run courses for members in working creatively with conflict.

Die Schule für Verständigung und Mediation (the School for Communication and Mediation) was created to share with the wider world the mediation technologies developed in the Lebensgarten ecovillage in Germany. These included non-violent communication and conflict facilitation practices that are now commonly used in the workplace and in negotiations of all types, but that were somewhat radical and pioneering when the School was established in 1990. Today, the School has developed a partnership with the Bremer Volkshochschule, a 'folk university', and issues formally accredited diplomas. It also operates as a consultancy, taking mediation techniques honed in the ecovillage into business and the trade unions.

Similarly, the Findhorn Foundation Consultancy was created with the aim of sharing the skills developed within the ecovillage to build community, facilitate decision-making and work with conflict. It undertakes organisation development together with mentoring and training in fields such as Appreciative Inquiry, leadership training, group-building and conflict facilitation. Clients include colleges, non-profit organisations (including Greenpeace International and AOPEB, an association of more than 30,000 Bolivian farmers that is moving into fair trade and organic markets) and businesses (among them BP, Shell, GlaxoSmithKline and PricewaterhouseCoopers).

Social inclusion

An important dimension of the ecovillage goal to create vibrant, self-governing communities is the impulse to promote social inclusion. Visitors from the economically rich countries to countries of the South are generally struck by the wealth, health and vitality of community life they find there. The elders are available as a source of wisdom and continuity. Children are looked after by a host of family members and friends. Those with disabilities and special needs tend to be woven in as valued members of the community. The contrast with the 'richer' countries could hardly be greater.

Ecovillages in the North act as laboratories and pioneers of forms of social organisation that permit a reweaving of the social fabric. To some extent, this has been an organic development from the decision to downsize and simplify, thus leaving more time to spend in community with others. In a number of cases, however, it is at the heart of the ecovillage's very *raison d'être*.

The Icelandic ecovillage Sólheimar, for example, was created in the 1930s as an experiment in de-institutionalising special needs children.

Founded by Sesselja H. Sigmundsdóttir, who was fascinated by the vision and theories of Rudolf Steiner, Sólheimar is today a vibrant and innovative community providing myriad opportunities for special needs and non-special needs people to work, live and play together.

Residents choose to work in one of a number of businesses: art workshop, ceramics studio, weaving studio, herbal soap factory, candle factory, wood workshop, organic tree nursery and reforestation project, organic farm, a hotel, café and restaurant and a general store and crafts shop. There is also a strong emphasis on theatre, visual arts and music. The Sólheimar's theatre group, founded in 1931, is the only group in the country where actors with special needs work alongside those without special needs on an equal basis.

Another initiative within the ecovillage family that has sought to pioneer a more socially inclusive model is the Kitezh community, 300 km south-west of Moscow. As with Sólheimar, the aim at Kitezh is to de-institutionalise the marginalised, in this case orphans, by integrating them into a loving community. The Kitezh project was launched in 1992 by Dimitri Morozov who left his job as a radio journalist in Moscow and inspired others to join him in the countryside to build a community for children.

The local administration gave them 100 hectares of land left vacant since the collapse of the collective farm system. They began work, building houses and vegetable gardens, a school, a farm and a church. Work is now underway on a second community, Orion, 70 km south of Moscow. Reed-bed waste-water wetland systems have been built at Kitezh and Orion to improve the quality of water that runs into local streams.

Kitezh also runs summer camps for orphans from regional orphanages and a therapeutic programme for emotionally troubled children from middle-class families who live in Kitezh for a period, benefiting from the healing environment. Kitezh's ambitions have grown. Having demonstrated the value of the model it has pioneered, the community is seeking to facilitate a network of family-based Children's Villages all over Russia.

In 2003, Kitezh was officially recognised as a therapeutic education community when it became the first international associate member of the Charterhouse Group of Therapeutic Communities in the UK.

One final example of ecovillage-inspired social inclusion activism comes from The Farm ecovillage in Tennessee. Members of The Farm community made contact with a group of urban pioneers called 'Sweat Equity', engaged in the heroic enterprise of refurbishing abandoned housing for the poor in the Bronx. Inspired by this example, The Farm created and funded an ambulance service for emergency care and transport for residents of the South Bronx from 1978 until 1984.

Out of this initiative was born the Kids to the Country programme, whose mission is "to create a multicultural exchange in a rural setting for at-risk children, build a positive sense of community through non-violent conflict resolution skills, and promote the growth of healthful relationships with each other". In the summer programme the kids spend time in nature, learn conflict management, make crafts, participate in recycling and gardening, make solar cookers, perform on stage and bond with new friends. Some 100 of Nashville's most at-risk children come to The Farm every year.

Peace activism and international solidarity

Peace activism and international solidarity also lie at the heart of the ecovillage ethic: concerns over war and global justice have inspired the creation of many communities. Alliances, exchanges and twinning relationships abound within the network. Some are especially worthy of note.

Sarvodaya, the largest single member of GEN (it works with around 15,000 villages across Sri Lanka) was an active player in brokering the peace agreement that ended the civil war that raged in Sri Lanka for thirty years: its Peace Meditation in Colombo in 1999 drew 170,000 participants. More recently, it has been engaged in the post-tsunami clean-up and reconstruction. Money to support these efforts has poured into Sarvodaya (and also into Auroville for similar clean-up work) from the ecovillage family worldwide, while Crystal Waters ecovillage in Australia also sent engineers to help Sarvodaya plan its post-tsunami strategy.

The Farm ecovillage has laid great emphasis on international solidarity and peace work. In 1974, Plenty International was founded as an outreach arm for the community. At first, Plenty just gave away surplus food from The Farm's own production to the local rural poor. Food aid was sent farther afield as the community discovered pockets of hunger in urban Nashville, Memphis, Chicago, rural Alabama and Mississippi. When a devastating earthquake struck Guatemala in 1976, killing 23,000 and leaving a million homeless, Plenty committed crews of carpenters to assist the Mayans in their efforts to rebuild. Over the next four years, Plenty volunteers built more than 1,200 houses, schools and public buildings. This led to the construction of a Mayan-owned and operated soy dairy (Alimentos San Bartolo) that is still in business today.

Plenty extends training and information in the specialised field of soybean agriculture and use in many countries across the world. In 1991 it launched a Soybean Utilization Training Assistance Program (SUP) in response to numerous requests from groups in Africa, Asia, the Caribbean and Latin America and is today a major player in the Central American Food Security Initiative.

Most recently, Plenty has been involved in relief and recovery operations in the wake of Hurricane Katrina, including home repair and clean-up, training of locals in roofing repair, provision of food, clothing and cleaning supplies and medical care. In 1980, Plenty was a recipient of the first Right Livelihood Award.

Also based at The Farm is the PeaceRoots Alliance, an organisation dedicated to fostering peace through non-violent means, whose programmes include 'Farms Not Arms', that campaigns for war-related expenditures to be channelled towards initiatives that address hunger and disease by supporting small farmers around the world; and Conscientious Objectors, a programme providing guidance and instruction for young people wishing to establish their status as conscientious objectors.

The ecovillage of Tamera in Portugal describes itself as a 'healing biotope'—a 'research centre for lived peace'. At the heart of its mission is the creation of a network of similar centres worldwide that will contribute to the establishment of a 'global healing field'. Over the last five years, it has fostered the development of a network of peace activists in Israel and Palestine, a number of whom have come to study in Tamera. In early 2005, Tamera co-founder Sabine Lichtenfels gave away all her possessions and set off penniless on a pilgrimage from Germany to Israel to promote 'The Humanisation of Money'—"the need to invest as much in peace as we currently do in war".

She was joined by a further fifty Israelis, Palestinians and international pilgrims, on a walk for peace through Israel and the occupied territories under the slogan "We Refuse to be Enemies". This included performances of a theatre piece of the same name and a mass meditation on November 9, anniversary of Kristalnacht in 1938 and of the collapse of the Berlin Wall in 1989. The next stage will be the building of a peace village in Israel/Palestine.

Tamera is also working closely with the village of San José de Apartadó and a network of twelve other 'peace villages' in Colombia. These villages have responded to the brutal civil war that rages around them—and that has seen a good number of their inhabitants murdered—by declaring themselves neutral in the conflict.

Their aim, with Tamera's support, is to become a network of ecovillages for peace, centres that demonstrate non-violence and ecological sustainability as a response to the war. It is less likely that these villages will be attacked by bandits if Europeans are staying there, as their deaths would attract unfavourable international media attention. A team of Tamera ecovillagers is preparing to provide this support. Hermann Scheer, holder of a Right Livelihood Award and founder of the Europe-wide initiative for sustainable energies, 'Eurosolar', has agreed to help design the plans for the San José 'solar village', and there will be exchange visits between Tamera and San José, culminating in the transfer of solar technologies in late 2006.

For the last two years, the Italian ecovillage Comune di Bagnaia has also been active in peace work involving Israelis and Palestinians. The community has been receiving young people coming on peace camps organised by the Israeli-Palestinian organisation Windows: Channels for Communication, as a way of enabling young people in the region to get to know and befriend each other. The camps used to be held in Israel until, following the outbreak of the *intifada*, it became impossible for people to move freely between Israel and the occupied territories.

Bagnaia offered the ecovillage as a meeting place, an offer that Windows was happy to accept. The young people talk and work together in Bagnaia, guided by facilitators, during the day, and lodge with local families by night. Those who have participated in the peace camps at Bagnaia said that the entire experience—often involving difficult and painful learning experiences—is greatly enhanced by the fact that the camps are held within the context of a living community. One peace camp costs around €20,000 to host and Bagnaia has succeeded in raising this from local foundations and other donors.

Out of the great range of possible ecovillage-based international solidarity initiatives that could be described, just a few more examples will be given here. The charity Bikes For Senegal is the inspiration of ecovillagers in Denmark. Besides sending more than 2,500 bikes to the COLUFIFA organisation (see the case study on Faoune in Chapter 2 for more details) along with two complete sets of workshop equipment to maintain them, Bikes for

Senegal has also sent large numbers of sewing machines, typewriters, wheelchairs and spectacles, plus medical equipment. Yet all this material assistance is just one facet of a relationship that is just as much about mutual learning and cultural exchange. Many people from Denmark have visited COLUFIFA since 1997, to work, to study or simply for a biking holiday. And many people from COLUFIFA have been to Denmark, to attend folk high schools or take part in cross-cultural dialogues. Bikes for Senegal has arranged three inter-religious dialogues on the topic of peace for participants from the two countries.

The Ladakh Project performs a similar function in promoting a healthy meeting of equals between people from North and South. Ladakhi community leaders are sponsored to come to the North on 'reality tours', which serve to balance the glamourised image of modern, urban life that is spread through advertising, television and tourism. Such experiences enable the Ladakhis to make more informed choices about their own future. Meanwhile, the Tourism for Change Program has been created to sensitise tourists to their impact during their stay in Ladakh and give them guidelines for culturally, economically and ecologically responsible behaviour. The Project has also published a 'counter-development' comic book, *A Journey to New York*, which is used in schools throughout Ladakh.

Collaboration between the Ecovillage at Ithaca and colleagues in Senegal led to the decision to locate the Third International Ecocities Conference in the Senegalese fishing town of Yoff and, eventually, the creation of the Senegalese Ecovillage Network. Training and other support provided by the Italian ecovillage Torri Superiori contributed to the formation of the Balkan ecovillage network, with members from throughout the former Yugoslavia. This promises to be an important player in helping to heal the wounds opened by the recent civil war. The School for Communication and Mediation at Lebensgarten has also been working since 1994 with partners in Croatia, where it has supported the birth of Croatia's Eco-Center Latinovac that provides mediation services.

Finally, the Nordic Energy Folkecenter, one of the founder members of the Danish ecovillage network and among the great research and demonstration eco-centres in Europe, has devoted much energy to sharing its expertise with poorer parts of the world. It has, for example, provided technical expertise to the Mali-Folkecenter in the fields of renewable energy technologies, the delivery of enterprise development services to small rural enterprises, and energy and environment policy work with the Malian government.

Holistic, whole person education

The area in which ecovillages have perhaps had greatest success in creating bridges to mainstream society is in the area of education. This forms the bedrock of many ecovillage economies.

Until relatively recently, most ecovillage education has been non-formal in nature, with individuals paying to attend generally non-accredited courses independent of any official school or college-based programme. Courses of this nature cover a wide range of subjects, including permaculture and ecovillage design, renewable energy systems, art and crafts, performance arts and spirituality.

Freed from the constraints of conventional educational structures and pedagogies and given the availability of the entire community as a grand social and technical laboratory and classroom, ecovillages have become masters in the design and delivery of this type of educational package. Many have won national and international recognition as centres of excellence, and awards have followed.

To name but a few, Kibbutz Lotan received the Israeli Ministry of the Environment's 2000 Shield award for work in environmental education. Ecocentro IPEC (Instituto de Permacultura e Ecovilas do Cerrado) in Brazil has won multiple awards, including the prestigious Banco do Brasil prize for the development of dry compost toilet and water tank technologies, and the Casa Claudia award for innovative design in natural construction. The Ecovillage Training Center at The Farm won recognition from the US National Sustainability Council for three consecutive years, and was twice awarded prizes by the National Gardening Association for its work with children. Ecological Solutions, an educational business in Australia's Crystal Waters ecovillage, won the 2001 Sunshine Coast Environmental Council award for its Eco-training Centre.

One of the most colourful and creative experiments in non-formal education is that conducted by La Caravana del Arcoiris por la Paz (The Rainbow Caravan of Peace), an itinerant community of around twenty people from close to ten different nationalities that travels around Central and South America in its small fleet of trucks, teaching permaculture, sustainability and issues relating to civil rights. Created by two ecovillage activists from the Mexican ecovillage, Huehuecoyotl, La Caravana's medium of communication is the arts: the community is made up of actors, dancers, musicians, jugglers and other performers. Created in 1996, La Caravana has worked in nineteen countries, spending much time working with the poor in indigenous villages and in inner-city barrios. In 2000, La Caravana was recognised by the Ecovillage Network of the Americas as a 'mobile ecovillage'.

A European sister initiative is the Travelling School of Life. This EU-funded initiative offers young people the opportunity to travel between ecovillages in central and eastern Europe, learning skills in organic gardening, community building and various eco-technologies.

One or two ecovillages also have longstanding relationships with formal educational bodies. The most prominent of these is CAT (which began life as a community and, even if most of its members have now moved off-site, is still an active member of GEN-Europe), which hosts up to 70,000 visitors a year, many of them schoolchildren.

More recently, there has been a significant and exciting increase in cooperation between ecovillages and colleges of further and higher education. Increasingly, the latter are coming to recognise the value of ecovillages as centres of education that synthesise theoretical and applied learning within the context of living communities.

CAT may be the first ecovillage to successfully set up a collaborative programme with a mainstream university. It teaches students on the University of East London's MSc in Architecture: Advanced Environmental and Energy Studies. In the first year that CAT participated in this programme, it had fifteen students. Seven years later, it now has more than 200. CAT is to be the home of the Wales Institute for Sustainable Education (WISE), a regional centre of expertise that will come into being over the next few years.

Similarly, having begun life as a non-formal training centre, the Brazilian institute IPEC has now developed collaborative relationships with universities in Brazil as well as in Spain, United States and Puerto Rico. Additionally, IPEC has launched the exciting new 'Sustainable School' programme, whose aim is to give students, parents and teachers the skills they need to create sustainable school campuses.

As we have seen, Ecovillage at Ithaca has also become an important educational resource and partner with numerous colleges and universities. A growing swell of postgraduate students worldwide are basing their research projects on ecovillage activities.

Another interesting bridge between ecovillages and universities is the US-based organisation Living Routes, founded in 1999 to help students at US universities learn how to build a sustainable future. Since then, semester and other shorter programmes have been developed at Auroville, Findhorn, Huehuecoyotl in Mexico, EcoYoff in Senegal, Ecoversidade in Brazil, Sirius in the US and the high Amazon of Peru. All courses are offered for college credit through the University of Massachusetts–Amherst. Around 400 students have been through ecovillage-based Living Routes programmes. New programmes are planned with ecovillages in Brazil, Israel and the US.

The long-term vision of Living Routes is to create a 'communiversity', an accredited school through which students would spend time and take courses in a variety of ecovillages and other innovative organisations around the world and earn a degree in sustainable living. Students could specialise in areas such as whole systems design, ecological building, holistic health, appropriate technologies, community-scale governance and decision-making and so on.

Cooperation between GEN and UNITAR (United Nations Institute for Training and Research) over the last seven years is also now becoming formalised in the shape of a joint programme. UNITAR has, since 1999, been a sponsor of the Findhorn Foundation's annual Ecovillage Training Programme, which brings together up to forty professionals, academics and activists from around the world on a month-long course. On the basis of this cooperation, over the last several years, ecovillage modules have been integrated into the training programmes run by UNITAR's CIFAL (French acronym for International Training Centre for Local Authorities) programme: GEN representatives have been involved in teaching sustainability-related courses to mayors and other local government officials in CIFAL centres in Durban, Curitiba, Kuala Lumpur and Ouagadougou. Today, the Findhorn Foundation ecovillage is becoming a new node in the CIFAL network of training centres, with special responsibility for developing courses on sustainability for officials from small towns and cities.

Over the last several years, a team of ecovillage educators, working under the name of Gaia Education and comprising educators from every continent, has been designing a standard ecovillage training curriculum, drawing upon best practice in ecovillages internationally in the fields of ecology, economy, spirituality and the social dimension of sustainability. This curriculum, under the name of Ecovillage Design Education (EDE), was formally launched in October 2005 and has been endorsed by UNESCO as an important element of the UN Decade of Education for

Sustainable Development. The programme is being field-tested in numerous ecovillages and other training centres.

Another ecovillage educational initiative that is worthy of note is the recently launched Gaia University. The brainchild of two senior ecovillage educators, Gaia University offers students the opportunity to gain academic qualifications by using a self-directed, action learning methodology that permits the undertaking of more experiential and hands-on learning projects than would be possible in conventional universities. Beginning in 2006, the first Gaia University Regional Center, Gaia Center for Education and Research, will open at The Farm ecovillage in Tennessee.

Even La Caravana is building bridges with mainstream institutions. It has been invited to be a key player in a new initiative launched by Gilberto Gil, Brazil's Secretary of Culture. The idea is to promote a flowering of traditional and contemporary community cultural centres across Brazil, and La Caravana has been built into the design as a key resource. In the words of Caravana elder and spokesman Alberto Ruz, their role will be "to weave among those centers, sharing our experience in the local communities, and taking from each one of them aspects of their own specific work, to help support and promote the preservation of the rich diversity of cultures that co-exist in this nation".

Conclusions

The first impression to leap from the page is the sheer energy and creativity at play here. Ecovillages are pioneering new models on multiple fronts. One is struck by how often they are in the vanguard in introducing new technologies or models—organic agriculture, CSAs, building techniques, mixed special needs and non-special needs groups, community currencies, solar technologies, biological waste-water treatment plants and so on— that subsequently become more widely adopted in society at large.

It is clear that there are ecovillage attributes that enable them to move more quickly and boldly in the introduction of innovations than other change agents. Their small scale and shared values clearly serve them well. Of equal importance, however, is the community dimension. There are so many challenges that face us today on the path to sustainability that cannot be addressed at the level of the individual or even the small group, and for which community-level action is required. CSA agriculture, biological waste-water treatment systems, community currencies, Earth restoration projects, re-weaving the marginalised back into the social fabric: all these become viable propositions only with a critical mass of people.

One final insight to emerge from the last two chapters concerns the nature of ecovillages themselves. What is interesting is that with few exceptions—Auroville, Damanhur, Findhorn, perhaps one or two others—none of the intentional communities described here is anywhere near large enough to truly be described as a 'village'. There is a reasonable number of what might be called 'eco-hamlets' of around 100 or so people, but very few true villages. Moreover, the initiatives we have been describing feel, above all, like community-based research, training and demonstration centres rather than villages in any conventional sense. The choice to go to live in a Northern ecovillage tends to be based on the desire to align oneself with specific values and in service of a broad cause, or action research project.

This is a useful insight that helps us further distinguish between ecovillages and other more mainstream communities, even those that have a good number of residents who are concerned and engaged environmentalists within them. Ecovillages can be likened to yoghurt culture: small, dense and rich concentrations of activity whose aim is to transform the nature of that which surrounds them.

Chapter 4

Challenges

We can't solve problems by using the same kind of thinking we used when we created them.—Albert Einstein

Watching the footage of the various events in the mid-1990s where GEN was created and formally launched, one could not fail to be moved by the ebullient optimism of the Network's founders. The ecovillage concept appeared, in the words of GEN co-creator, Albert Bates, "to have the winds of inevitability at its back": the first GEN T-shirt boldly declared "Welcome To The Future!"

Given the many achievements of the last decade, much progress has undoubtedly been made. Nonetheless, it is also true that ecovillages remain largely peripheral to the mainstream debate in today's societies, which show little inclination to take serious strides towards sustainability. In the recent Sustainable Communities consultation in the UK, for example, GEN remained below the government's radar and none of the official case studies presented as 'ecovillages' or 'sustainable communities' in the media came anywhere close to meeting the criteria used by GEN: most were large settlements whose innovative design features were limited to the technological.

Moreover, while there has been some growth in the number of ecovillages over the last ten years, this has been rather slow, falling short of the hopes of GEN's founders. So, despite the vitality and creativity that is so evident from the various initiatives described, the ecovillage family still faces many challenges, external and internal.

External challenges

Let us look first at the economically rich countries of the North. Here, it is incontestable that the job of creating and maintaining an ecovillage has become substantially more difficult over the last couple of decades. This is for two main reasons. First, globalisation has facilitated an increased flow of cheap, mass-produced goods (often carrying hidden subsidies and including few social and ecological externalities). This has undermined efforts at promoting small-scale, locally based economies of the type that ecovillages seek to build, making it ever more difficult for them to identify economic niches in which they have a comparative advantage. In parallel, also in part as a result of macro-economic policies, land prices have risen, often sharply, in most countries of the North. Both these factors make it more difficult for ecovillages to form and prosper.

A second and parallel trend has been the tightening of the regulatory framework in such a way as to make ecovillages, and other efforts at citizen-led community development, significantly more difficult. The process of winning approval for the building of new settlements and individual houses, for example, especially where innovative, non-traditional settlements are planned, has become enormously more fraught. By way of example, the Findhorn Foundation community had to go through a similar planning process for permission to erect three windmills in early 2006 as would have the developer of a wind-farm. This meant that more money was spent in gaining permission for the new turbines than in their acquisition, transport and installation!

Regulations around banking and community currencies have also been tightened, making it much more difficult for community initiatives to flourish. Thus, for example, the Ecological Building Society was formed in 1981 with capital assets of £5,000. Today, the creation of a bank within the European Union requires minimum capital of five million Euros, thus making it all but impossible for communities to take this route. The largest single item of expenditure in the creation of Findhorn's 'community bank' (legally, an Industrial and Provident Society) and community currency (legally, 'book tokens') was fees for lawyers to seek loopholes in the legislation.

Perhaps most seriously of all for ecovillages, food-processing at the village scale as an economic activity has become all but impossible. George Monbiot describes the situation in the UK with his usual insight: "There are two sets of regulations . . . those which the big corporations campaign against, and those which they tolerate and even encourage, because they can afford them while their smaller competitors cannot. This is why it is legal to stuff our farm animals with antibiotics, our vegetables with pesticides, our processed food with additives and our water tables with nitrates, but more or less illegal to use any process which does not involve stainless steel, refrigeration and fluorescent lighting." The minimum investment required for food-processing today has driven many small-scale enterprises out of business.

Taken together, these two factors have inhibited the establishment of new ecovillages and restricted the development of those already on the ground. A solid majority of ecovillages in the countries of the North remain small, with a clear majority having fewer than fifty members. In some cases, they stay small because this is their members' choice. More frequently, the regulatory framework imposes a glass ceiling that only the most clever, determined and lucky are able to break through.

An important consequence is that many ecovillages remain too small to be of much value as research, demonstration and training centres. There are no absolutes here: some micro-communities of fewer than twenty members have been highly effective as change agents far beyond their own boundaries. Nonetheless, as a general rule, the smaller the community, the less scope there is for functional specialisation and the more time members need to spend simply keeping the operation afloat.

Meanwhile, the trend towards greater global economic integration—with all the concentrations of wealth and power that this entails—leaves ecovillages in the North even further away from the 'mainstream' political dialogue than they already were. The ecovillage spokesman in dialogue with policy-makers and planners is increasingly left with little recourse other than: "I really would not start from here!", the well-worn lament of all change-agents seeking to address an old paradigm from within the thought patterns of the new.

Life for ecovillages in the countries of the South has also become more difficult as a result of the trends towards greater globalisation. Three factors are at play. First, ever-larger areas are being taken out of community control and food production for local needs into plantation agriculture for the global market and tourism. This impacts on community access to and control over land, water and food. Except in those pockets where export crops predominate (and in some cases, not even there), impoverishment grows and working-age people are sucked into the urban slums.

Second, the tentacles of the global media have greatly increased their reach, carrying messages glamourising consumerism and undermining traditional values and lifestyles into all but the most isolated communities. Third, global warming and other forms of ecological degradation are having a disproportionately heavy impact among poor communities of the South. This generates waves of environmental refugees that, as we saw in the case of Mbam ecovillage in Senegal in Chapter 2, then overwhelm communities that may have found ways of living in some sort of balance within their ecosystems. Together, these factors have made it progressively more difficult for communities in the South to find ways of living sustainably.

One final externally generated challenge worthy of mention is a drift towards greater individualism in society at large that is in turn mirrored within ecovillages themselves. The consequences of this in terms of the vitality and capacity of ecovillages are discussed under the category of internal challenges.

Internal challenges

As noted in the two preceding chapters, ecovillages are active on many different fronts and, indeed, this profusion of creative activity is a defining characteristic and source of strength: ecovillages, after all, seek to be multi-dimensional settlements rather than sectoral specialists. However, it is also arguable that this very wealth of diversity—in terms of the range of both activities and the forms that ecovillages take—also acts to dilute their power and profile.

Chapter 2 identified five common characteristics of all ecovillages—they are:

- private citizens' initiatives
- in which the communitarian impulse is of central importance
- that are seeking to win back some measure of control over community resources
- that have a strong shared values base (sometimes referred to as 'spirituality'), and
- that act as centres of research, demonstration and (in most cases) training.

However, such is the diversity of expression of these principles that many initiatives may feel only secondary allegiance to the ecovillage family. It is likely, for example, that Camphill communities or ecovillages such as

Sólheimar and Kitezh will locate themselves primarily within the family of socially inclusive care organisations, that Sarvodaya's primary alliances will be with other South Asian development organisations, and that communities with a highly distinctive esoteric mission, such as Damanhur, may prioritise their relations with their own international affiliated offshoots over all others. In each of these cases, and perhaps in many others, the commonality of interest felt with the ecovillage network—either informally or formally, in the shape of GEN—may not be sufficiently strong to make it effective as a collective body or movement.

Of course, this in no way diminishes the value or significance of the work that each ecovillage is undertaking in its own locality or within its family of primary allegiance. It is, however, likely to weaken the value of the ecovillage concept as a unifying symbol and to dilute the clarity and power of organisations, such as GEN, that purport to represent this wide and divergent family. This seems to some degree unavoidable.

A similar challenge is posed by the great diversity in the forms that ecovillages take. The range in the type, size and nature of initiatives described in this book could hardly be greater. This is not necessarily a problem in itself until one considers the challenge of replication: those asking innocently, "How does one create an ecovillage?" rarely find a simple and useful answer. There can be little doubt that one of the major reasons that ecovillages have not proliferated to the degree hoped for and anticipated over the last decade is the lack of templates for would-be ecovillagers to follow. The creation of such templates is one of the major tasks facing the ecovillage movement and we will return to this in the last chapter.

As we have seen, being citizens' initiatives, ecovillages enjoy great freedom to act radically and quickly—or as quickly as consensual decision-making permits! This does, however, also have a down-side: ecovillages, especially those in the countries of the North, have very limited access to official sources of funding and tend to be largely dependent on private resources. Given this fact, it is astonishing that ecovillages have been able to achieve as much as they have. Substantial amounts of money have been raised from within ecovillages and from the networks of friends and supporters of their values and projects. This is in large part down to the creative acumen that ecovillagers bring to the art of fundraising. However, this drains time and resources that could be spent more creatively. It also imposes a limit on what can be achieved: many great ideas for projects in ecovillages never see the light of day, or fail to achieve their full potential, due to a lack of finance.

The trend towards greater individualism and a weakening of the communal impulse within ecovillages has been mentioned above. This finds expression in an increased trend for individuals—rather than the collective body—to build houses, demands by members for more private space, a loosening of the common economy, a higher turnover of members and, arguably, a weakening of the value base that acts as the social 'glue' of many communities.

The Svanholm ecovillage in Denmark provides an example of how this plays out in practice. In 1978, a group of eighty-five adults and forty-five children bought a manor house and assorted buildings surrounded by an estate of 1,025 acres. The community ethic was profoundly egalitarian and self-sufficient, and from the start great emphasis was laid on converting the farm to organic production. Quickly, the community became largely self-reliant in food. The collective also looked after the renovation and conversion of the buildings. Around one third of the members worked outside the community but all income was pooled and the community association provided food, accommodation, seaside homes for holidays together with money to enable members to take sabbaticals and for other occasional expenditures. Most members who joined the community expected to spend the rest of their lives there.

Today, the community has shrunk to about two-thirds of its original size—sixty adults and thirty children—primarily as a result of members requiring greater private space. A loan has been taken out to build new accommodation to enable the population to grow back to close to its original size. The community has an ageing population, due in part to the difficulty of attracting young people to participate in the common economy system. This has now been weakened so that members can keep twenty per cent of their income, and the community provides fewer common services than before. Turnover of members has increased and, arguably, commitment to values of voluntary simplicity, self-reliance and life-long commitment to the community have weakened.

With some notable exceptions, these trends are echoed more or less across the board within ecovillages and other intentional communities. In some respects, this may be considered to be no bad thing: ecovillages, as a result, are likely to be more attractive to more mainstream people. But there is a price to be paid. In very practical terms, when individuals take over the building of homes, the many potential benefits of common design features are much harder to realise: shared district boilers, common wetland waste-treatment facilities, solar energy generation and other technologies that are viable only above a certain scale are much more likely to be built into the design of whole settlements—or clusters—than into that of individual houses.

Moreover, growing disparities among members in terms of income and in the size and quality of housing is almost bound to impact on feelings of solidarity within communities. The same is true of the increased ease of air travel and the growth in rootlessness, which is reflected in higher turnover of members. This is certainly one factor explaining the demographic challenge facing many ecovillages, with the pioneering generation of many of the larger ecovillages created in the 1960s and 1970s ageing, and insufficient numbers of young people coming through to replace them.

Despite these trends, most ecovillages continue to have core groups of highly committed, long-term members and to exude a strong sense of purpose and shared values. However, this progressive weakening of the core communitarian impulse must be considered as one of the principal reasons explaining the relative paucity of newly created large and successful ecovillages in recent years.

One final challenge facing ecovillages is that of becoming less insular and more enmeshed in the fabric of their own bioregions. Given the high levels of outreach and engagement with the world described in the previous two chapters, this may seem a puzzling assertion. Nonetheless, it remains true that many ecovillages are only marginally anchored within their own bioregions. There appear to be two dimensions to this. The first is the question of scale already alluded to: small ecovillages have so few hands and are so busy just staying afloat that there is little spare capacity for service to a wider cause—local or otherwise.

Second, ecovillages often find themselves caught between the present requirement to cater to the needs of their consumer base or ideological allies (those, often living far away, paying for their educational courses and consultancy services) and those of their immediate neighbours. This problem becomes exacerbated where neighbouring communities are unsympathetic, perhaps even hostile, and unaware of the potential value of the ecovillages in their midst.

This is a key challenge to ecovillages as we begin to make the transition to a more locally based world, propelled by the coming energy famine. The final chapter addresses the question of how ecovillages and governments alike can address the various challenges described here in order to release the full creative potential of ecovillages.

Chapter 5

Cutting Edges: ecovillages on the new frontiers of sustainability

I am reminded also of friends in several intentional communities and ecovillages around the world who have . . . decided to pursue Powerdown and lifeboat-building strategies simultaneously. While they engage in activism on many fronts—participating vigorously in the anti-globalisation, peace, and environmental movements—they also have established rural bases where they save heirloom seeds, build their own homes from natural and locally available materials and hone other life-support skills that they and future generations will need. I admire those people unreservedly: if there is a sane path from where we are to a truly sustainable future, these folks have surely found it.
—Richard Heinberg, Powerdown

To date, ecovillages have been swimming resolutely against the dominant socio-economic paradigm of our age—globalisation. Where globalisation is predicated on the notion that we can grow our way out of our social and ecological problems through ever-greater specialisation, accumulation and trade, ecovillages are the living manifestation of a philosophy of voluntary simplicity and greater self-reliance. Given that the dominant economic signals and regulatory frameworks so strongly favour mass-production and distribution and that ecovillages have benefited from so little official support, it is astonishing that they have been able to achieve as much as they have done.

There are, however, solid reasons for believing that the age of globalisation is coming to an end, perhaps even in the relatively short term. Most obviously, the long supply lines of products being transported hither and thither around the world—the ingredients of a typical British Sunday lunch have been calculated to travel up to 49,000 miles, a huge increase in recent years—are highly vulnerable to increases in fuel prices. Yet, with the imminent (perhaps already passed) peaking in the availability of oil, fuel prices are on the rise and appear bound to continue on this upward course. Large-scale plantation agriculture as it is currently practised is also very fossil fuel dependent.

Additionally, globalisation carries in its wake a range of other costs that appear unsustainable and at the root of numerous ecological crises. Climate change, the most serious of these, is directly linked to the large-scale, centralised industrial processes favoured by economic globalisation and to the emergence of settlement patterns and social structures that facilitate, even require, high levels of mobility. Industrial agriculture also mines the soil of nutrients, leading to erosion and loss of topsoil, draws water from underground aquifers in many part of the world at significantly greater than natural replenishment rates, and leaves a trail of pollution from chemical inputs.

In addition, the liberalisation of financial markets that has been such a driver of globalisation has created much greater volatility in the international system, leaving it markedly more vulnerable to shocks. All this is to say nothing of the social costs of a globalised system that, to date, has succeeded only in further polarising global differentials in wealth and power, driving peasant farmers off the land and creating a class of citizen so alienated from the dominant paradigm that it is prepared to take up arms against it.

Globalisation could be bankrupted by any one of these crises: the rise in fuel prices or in insurance damages associated with global warming; a drop in food supply due to a reduction in chemical inputs; decreased availability of water and/or loss of soil fertility; meltdown in the financial markets following a major debtor country default or some other generalised loss of confidence; and/or terrorist attacks on vital supply lines or other strategic targets. In each case, there is substantial evidence that we are moving ever closer to the edge of the cliff.

All this is profoundly worrying and appears to make it more or less inevitable that we are moving into a period of strife and suffering within the human family. However, it also means that our addiction to oil must be broken and that the kind of monopolistic economy we have today, with its devastating social and ecological consequences, will be left behind. There is much uncertainty about how the transition will unfold and over how long a period. It may be the result of a consciously chosen path of 'powering down' or, as looks progressively more likely, imposed upon us by a rupture that dislocates the entire system. Since we have never been here before, it is impossible to offer more than educated guesses on likely scenarios.

What does, however, appear inevitable is that human societies of the not too distant future will be more locally based and decentralised than those we know today. Society will have no choice but to take its foot off the accelerator pedal. The huge surpluses on which today's great concentrations of power and wealth are dependent will no longer be possible. Life must necessarily become simpler and more decentralised and, to survive, people will need to become more knowledgeable about their own bioregions.

However, and this is the great challenge that faces our civilisation, the last half-century or so has seen the dismantling of the very structures and knowledge base that people will need to survive and thrive through the transition. Sixty years ago, Britain was able to respond with vigour and imagination to the effective blockade imposed by war. The skills, technologies, community structures and shared values required for the rapid transition to high levels of self-sufficiency were still in place. This is no longer true today. The society that has since emerged is so little able to provide for any of its core needs—food, clothing, buildings, furniture and so on using locally available skills, resources and materials—that it finds itself much more vulnerable to external shock. We have combined three factors—extended supply lines, limited capacity to provide for our own needs and a growing number of external enemies—that are reminiscent of the last days of the Roman Empire.

The good news is that the types of applied research, demonstration and training that ecovillages are engaged in are precisely those that will be needed to navigate the rough waters ahead. Seen in this context, the initiatives that have been described on these pages—in reforestation, seed-saving, place-specific technologies for energy-efficient housing, food-growing, energy-generation, the development of inclusive decision-making structures, voluntary simplicity and so on—appear not so much idiosyncratic tinkering as the very stuff that the building of future societies will be made of.

Whether one is persuaded of the imminence of a cataclysmic global collapse or simply planning for making the transition to a world where we will need to provide for more of our own needs, it makes sense to ensure that as far as is possible, the wisdom, the models and the technologies developed within ecovillages are mobilised for the wider public good. However, it is not enough, as some ecovillagers appear to believe, to simply sit and wait for the new, decentralised, ecovillage-friendly world to appear. There are many dangers and pitfalls on the post-Peak Oil path that lies before us, and if ecovillages are to play an important role in facilitating the transition, both governments and ecovillages will need to work intelligently and cooperatively together.

New frontiers for ecovillages

Given the strong self-help ethic at the heart of ecovillages, it is fitting that we begin by looking first at the kinds of shifts that will be required within ecovillages themselves.

Ecovillages face three core challenges—and opportunities—as they seek to respond to the opportunities presented by the coming energy famine. The most important of these is that of enmeshing themselves more deeply within the fabric of their own bioregions. Thankfully, there is already a body of relevant precedent within the ecovillage family to draw ideas and inspiration from. We have already noted some of this above: the catalytic role played by Ecovillage at Ithaca within the local academic community and in the Sustainable Tompkins County initiative; Sieben Linden and ZEGG's place at the heart of emerging local networks of organic growers and suppliers; Auroville's work on medicinal plants with local communities in Tamil Nadu; and the role of The Farm, Sólheimar and others in local Earth restoration activities.

Three more especially interesting initiatives are described here as a way of illustrating how ecovillages could become more locally engaged. The first is the Ecodyfi initiative in Mid Wales, in which one of the leading players is the Centre for Alternative Technology (CAT). This is a broad alliance, comprising local authorities, community organisations and specialist agencies that is active in a range of areas and with CAT providing substantial technical expertise. Ecodyfi's mission is "to foster sustainable community regeneration in the Dyfi valley" in ways that are sustainable and that build on local distinctiveness: "Food, holiday and other products will all benefit from being associated with a clean, green image of the valley—where the Dyfi valley is a leader in sustainable community regeneration."

A key goal for Ecodyfi is to work towards 'greening' the local energy economy. Through an EU-funded project in 1998–2001, it brought around £300,000 into the local economy, raised local awareness of energy issues and implemented a number of small community-based water, wind, solar and wood-fuel schemes. These included the UK's first community-owned wind turbine, a farm-based hydro-electric scheme, and solar water heating in ten houses. Some income from the community-owned wind turbine is diverted to the Community Energy Fund to benefit energy conservation initiatives for local people. There are plans for a second community-owned wind turbine and for the development of biodiesel locally. Powys Renewable Energy Partnership, in which Ecodyfi is a central player, won the '100% Communities: Rural' category in a European Commission competition.

Ecodyfi is also an active partner in a number of programmes: to promote farm-scale horticultural production and marketing in the Dyfi Valley in partnership with the organisation Farming Connect; to strengthen community links through seed swaps, plant swaps and garden visits in collaboration with Dyfi Valley Seed Savers; to reduce waste and increase composting; to promote community-based tourism; to manage a wildlife area; to improve broadband access for local people; and to involve young people in the planning, design and fundraising for a sports facility for skateboarding, roller-blading and bicycles.

The Dyfi Biosphere Area has been accredited as the only UNESCO biosphere in Wales.

Ecodyfi also led a successful campaign for the Dyfi Valley to be uniquely awarded the status of Fair Trade Valley. Projects in the pipeline include a pilot project to introduce a community currency for the Dyfi Valley and the introduction of a wood-fuelled district heating system to heat one area of the valley in a carbon-neutral process.

By any standards, this is a prodigious list of achievements. For present purposes, two observations are in order. First, Ecodyfi did not emerge overnight, but rather as the culmination of many years of discussions between a gradually emerging loose coalition of organisations. Second, to be an effective partner in this coalition, CAT had to want to be of service to its home bioregion and to recognise that alone and in isolation from other local organisations, it could have achieved relatively little.

A second example of an ecovillage playing an effective and useful role of service to its own bioregion lies at the opposite end of the scale. The tiny Irish ecovillage, The Hollies, comprises only two full-time resident families, of which one member from both teaches at the further education college in the local town, Kinsale. One of these, Rob Hopkins, introduced the course, Practical Sustainability, as the world's first full-time, two-year permaculture course.

During the academic year 2004–2005, the students on this course worked on an 'energy descent' plan for Kinsale, exploring how the town could reduce its use of fossil fuels and become more self-sufficient. This process included a one-day seminar attended by many local people. The event included a showing of the DVD, *The End of Suburbia*, followed by a community think-tank to discuss issues raised by the film and brainstorm ideas about what could be done in the town to address them.

The end of the year saw the publication of a report, *Kinsale 2021: An Energy Descent Plan*, that included a long-term vision and a time-tabled strategy for descent in eleven key sectors: food, youth and community, education, housing, economy and livelihoods, health, tourism, transport, waste, energy and marine resources. This first phase of the project ended with a conference in June 2005 called 'Fuelling the Future—the challenge and opportunity of Peak Oil', in which some of the leading international figures in the field participated. The report and the conference were offered as "very firm first steps towards a more holistic way of approaching Kinsale's future".[2]

The model developed in Kinsale has proved highly inspirational to community initiatives worldwide. It is being imitated or used as a model by 'powerdown' initiatives in Edinburgh and Brighton and in the US in California, North Carolina, Colorado and Nevada.

One final case that is offered here as a source of ideas and inspiration is the ZEGG community, located south of Berlin. The community took over the training centre of STASI, the former East German secret police, and has devoted much energy into making the community an asset and resource for local regeneration. Having established the infrastructure of its own green technologies—including a biological waste-water treatment system, a CO_2 neutral community heating system fired by local wood-chips and organic food production—it launched a local promotion and information campaign to promote these technologies. This includes seminars, workshops, visitor days and articles in the regional newspapers. The community hosts regional days devoted to specific aspects of sustainable development in the region, including renewable energy and biodiesel.

In addition, ZEGG has participated in the creation of a local network of small organic farmers and bakeries that provide it with potatoes, eggs, bread, fruit and vegetables. It has been an active player in local initiatives to create a free-school, an infocafe, 'Der Winkel', which acts as a centre for tolerance against right-wing extremism and violence, projects with refugees

---

2. Rob Hopkins has since left The Hollies to return to his native England, but the Kinsale 2021 project continues under the guidance of his successor.

and asylum-seekers, a local exchange trading system, a forest kindergarten, campaigns to promote fair-trade products, community-supported-agriculture and all kinds of cultural activities.

It has also created a network of friendship, cooperation and support for other smaller communitarian projects in the region. This now meets several times a year and has grown to around 300 people, including many local residents. In 2005, it won the European Ecovillage Excellence Award for its ecological work in the region.

These three communities can be seen as pioneers on the path towards greater integration of ecovillages into their own bioregions. It is a lead that others need to follow if they are to be active participants in the coming social and economic relocalisation.

A second major challenge that ecovillages need to address concerns their difficulty of replication. Community activist Diana Leafe Christian was driven to write the seminal work, *Creating a Life Together: Practical Tools to Grow Ecovillages and Intentional Communities* by the observation that "Most aspiring ecovillage and community groups—probably 90 per cent—never get off the ground: their envisioned communities never get built." Now, it is certainly true that the steps involved in creating an ecovillage—identifying and building a core group, finding the land, working with the planning authorities, raising the investment capital, setting up a suitable legal structure, putting up buildings, agreeing on decision-making structures, how to make and distribute income, working with conflict and so on—are no small tasks. Nonetheless, the lack of commonly recognised templates or models too often means that each new group of would-be ecovillages are left to reinvent the wheel.

The cohousing movement appears to have much to teach in this respect. One important reason for its relatively rapid spread is that core models have been developed and this makes dialogue with planners much easier. It is unsurprising, then, to find that a number of recently established ecovillages have drawn on the cohousing model. This is most obviously the case with the Ecovillage at Ithaca in New York and Munksoegaard in Denmark, both of which formally describe themselves as cohousing ecovillages.

Here, the advantages of the cohousing model were apparent from the legal point of view: the authorities recognised, understood and supported what they were trying to do. Moreover, both communities are relatively conservative in economic terms and so the cohousing principle of avoiding any form of common economy posed no problem. Having found a convenient and already existing legal structure—thus saving themselves the time and resources required to invent a new one—both were then free to choose to be as radical as they wished in other areas.

Ecovillage at Ithaca has, in fact, developed a significantly stronger communitarian ethic than most conventional cohousing initiatives, hosting facilitated workshops for members on all kinds of topics from ecological footprinting, permaculture and sustainable investments, to non-violent communication, conflict facilitation and inclusive community-building. There is also a strong ethic of service within the community, especially in the field of sustainability education, and a relatively high proportion of the community—around sixty per cent—is employed at least part-time within the community.

The Village in Ireland, an initiative that is set to begin construction in 2006, also provides an interesting model that has strong potential to act as a template for future ecovillages. Members of the core group began meeting in Dublin in the late 1990s. However, they had the greatest difficulty in finding land with the requisite planning permission attached. Recognising that they would require the services of professionals to help them overcome this problem, they raised capital from within the group to employ a part-time worker to coordinate activities and an architect to help them work on a design.

The creation of the plan, together with the lobbying activities of their part-time employee, helped the group be taken more seriously and contributed to the eventual decision by North Tipperary County Council to rezone a piece of land, adjacent to the village of Cloughjordan, making it available for ecovillage development. This is a substantial plot of sixty-seven acres, on which the ecovillagers have permission to build around 100 serviced sites, community buildings, playgrounds, a network of cycle paths and walkways and significant agricultural land and a wildlife area.

These case studies point up several lessons. As planning regulations have tightened, it has become more difficult for groups to create substantial new settlements without professional assistance. One way around this, following the lead of The Village, is to pool risk capital from within the group to engage professionals to provide advice on legal and institutional advice and to help dialogue with the authorities. Having succeeded in getting permission in this way, nascent communities can then revert to more conventional ecovillage ways of building and managing the new settlement. Building work in The Village will predominantly be the responsibility of individuals, with some undertaking this on a self-build basis.

Second, it could greatly facilitate the start-up of new ecovillages for a small number of templates to be developed and catalogued, based on the circumstances and aspirations of several core categories of ecovillages. It looks as if the cohousing model could already serve the needs of some of these, and other category templates can be developed. The task for ecovillages is to analyse their requirements and to use existing legislation as far as possible, thus making life easier for the local government officials with whom they have to deal and saving on their own expenses.

One final point on the question of creating templates for ease of ecovillage replication. There is, within ecovillages, a strong anarchistic flavour, reflected among other ways in the desire for individuals to be involved in designing and building their own homes. It may be timely for ecovillages to question whether this luxury remains appropriate or affordable. There are several issues here. First, as noted above, there are many eco-efficient design features that work at the level of the settlement but not at the level of the individual house. Second, the unit costs of planning, designing and building together should be significantly lower for communal rather than individual builds.

Third, collectively planned building will permit more compact settlements with a lower footprint, as any who have visited BedZED will testify. This is an especially important consideration in the more densely populated parts of the world such as Western Europe and the coasts of North America. Fourth, and for all the above reasons, the model will be more easily recognised by official planners who will, in consequence, be more sympathetic to it.

It is true that building collectively requires a level of organisation—in terms of both raising capital and creating a central design—not required for individual house-building. However, what is being suggested here is that ecovillagers consider whether it is time to shed some of their individualistic tendencies in order to create more communal models that are cheaper, more socially inclusive, lighter in terms of impact and more replicable.

The final area where ecovillages may need to be more resourceful if they are to be able to respond in full to the opportunities arising out of the coming energy famine regards their self-financing strategies. We have already observed that the growth of many ecovillages is inhibited by some form of glass ceiling, with a lack of finance being an especially serious problem. Many potentially valuable ecovillage enterprises and initiatives never see the light of day because monies cannot be raised to finance them.

Yet there is a strong case to be made that ecovillage infrastructure projects offer among the safest and most useful investments available anywhere. If we could find a way of diverting funds out of conventional, stock market-based portfolios, perhaps along the lines being explored by the Norwegian Camphill communities (as described above in Chapter 3), this could go a long way towards providing capital for ecovillage projects.

Let us look at the case of pensions to see how an innovative ecovillage financing mechanism could work. Currently, some seventy-one per cent of UK pension funds (in the region of £530 billion) is invested in the stock market. However, this is profoundly lacking in precisely the kind of security that people past working age are looking for. The stock market is built on nothing other than investor confidence: it fell in value by forty-three per cent in the three years up to 2003, with UK pension funds falling in value by £250 billion in 2002 alone. While there has been an upturn since, the long-term trends already alluded to above hardly inspire confidence.

Ecovillage infrastructure projects, on the other hand, provide a solid asset backing for the investor. These could generate a stream of rental income paying long-term dividends to the investors. The trick would be to create 'Sustainability Pension Funds' that bring together into one portfolio projects at ecovillages (and perhaps other sister sustainability initiatives) that need financing and that could provide long-term rental returns. The task before the ecovillage family now is to find mechanisms that link up those wishing to save for a secure future with those who are in the process of creating it. Once again, intelligent thinking outside of conventional ecovillage spheres of influence is required.

New frontiers for government authorities

As ecovillages have richly demonstrated, much can be achieved with a minimum of official assistance. Nonetheless, it has also been noted that the tightening regulatory framework together with lack of access to official financing have acted as a significant brake on new and existing ecovillage developments.

The first step in addressing this is for government at national and local level to recognise the value of ecovillages as social and technological pioneers and as catalysts for regeneration. Today, in almost every corner of the world, communities are being sapped of their vitality. In the South, rural-urban drift takes the young out of the villages and into unsanitary slums. In the North, farming is in deep decline and villages are being taken over by dormitory populations or are being abandoned, while depressed inner cities areas become breeding grounds for crime. These are problems that ecovillages are expressly addressing. The community banks and currencies, the CSAs, the eco-technology enterprises, the community-based governance structures are precisely designed to breathe life back into depressed communities.

There is an obvious match here between the needs of government—at national and local levels—seeking to regenerate their local communities and the models developed by ecovillages to achieve just this aim. The greatest step that government can take towards facilitating this match is in creating new planning categories that favour the emergence of community-based centres that are researching, demonstrating and providing training on locally appropriate models for sustainable living.

This makes most obvious immediate sense in those areas that are already experiencing severe depopulation, including isolated areas of Spain, Italy and the west of Ireland and Scotland. Such thinking, indeed, appears to have influenced the decision on the part of Tipperary North Council to re-zone the land adjacent to Cloughjordan village for the new ecovillage development. Similarly, Byron Bay is one of several councils in Australia to have created an Ecovillage Zone within which ecovillages are permitted 'as of right'.

In no sense could such a more liberal attitude towards ecovillage development on the part of the planning authorities be seen as the 'writing of blank cheques'. In granting planning permission to The Village, the local authorities imposed twenty-five conditions that the development would need to meet, including several of an ecological nature.

In similar vein, the UK organisation Chapter 7 (created by Tinkers' Bubble resident Simon Fairlie), that campaigns to "provide access to land for all households through environmentally sound planning" proposes tight controls over dwellings and settlements that should be permitted. These include the following:

- The project has prepared a strategy for the minimisation of motor vehicle use.
- The project plans to minimise the creation of waste and to reuse and recycle as much as possible on site.
- The project has a strategy for energy conservation and the reduction, over time, of dependence on non-renewable energy sources to a practical minimum.
- The project can demonstrate that no activities pursued on the site shall cause undue nuisance to neighbours or the public.

The introduction of such conditions, together with the setting of a review period, would make this a low-risk strategy for local authorities, with the potential to deliver substantial tangible benefits. Moreover, given that we are referring here to ecovillages primarily as regional R&D and training centres, the proposal is not that local authorities necessarily respond favourably to proposals for a large number of ecovillage projects in their areas. It may well be appropriate, initially at least, to create an opportunity for one per region (how this is defined remains up for question) and to give approval to the proposal that looks likely to best meet the needs of the area in question.

A more ambitious scheme would be for government to make vacant brown-field sites available for ecovillages under the legal form of land trusts. The land trust model—whereby the land is granted by the government on condition that it be taken out of the future sale value of the property, thus keeping it in perpetuity as affordable housing stock—is already being considered by the government as a way of helping low-income key workers such as nurses and teachers onto the bottom rung of the housing market.

The process of globalisation is seeing the transfer of many jobs and industries out of the countryside. This is freeing up land and former workspaces, some of it owned by the government. Some of these facilities could be transferred to ecovillage initiatives.

Government can also facilitate ecovillage access to financing in three different ways. First, the proposal to create Sustainability Pension Funds draws heavily on a recent New Economics Foundation policy paper called *Peoples' Pension Funds*. The idea is that government and the banking industry cooperate to create a new tier of pension funds, enabling people to invest in community infrastructure projects—schools, hospitals, community centres etc.—with long-term rental income from these facilities supplying the pension dividends. The Sustainability Pension Funds would operate along similar lines and would greatly benefit from the introduction of legislation permitting the model proposed in the NEF policy paper.

Second, local authorities could help promote and participate in community currency schemes, such as those initiated by ecovillages. There is a growing body of evidence demonstrating the potential of community currencies to regenerate local economies, and there is obvious scope for local authorities in promoting their more widespread use.

Finally, there are many areas—especially in the implementation of Local

Agenda 21 programmes—where ecovillages and local authorities are natural partners. Given their long experience in developing models for sustainability with a minimum of external funding, ecovillages have become masters in both community mobilisation and getting value for money. Central and local government are coming under greater pressure to achieve environmental targets: for recycling, renewable energy-generation, reduced emissions and so on. These are all areas in which ecovillages have location-specific expertise. There is an obvious rationale behind pulling them in as fully paid-up partners in the design and implementation of sustainable community development strategies.

Within its historical context, the choice made by ecovillages to follow a highly alternative path to that of mainstream society is understandable. Within the mainstream, it would have been all but impossible to create microcosmic societies of the type that the ecovillagers dreamed of. Moreover, the very act of stepping out of the predominant paradigm to participate in creating a new one had the magic of boldness about it. Ecovillages have gained greatly in confidence by demonstrating their ability to take power into their own hands.

The world is now on the point of a great turning. The coming energy famine means that communities will have little choice but to relocalise along the lines that ecovillages have been pioneering. While in some respects, ecovillages remain highly distinctive, in others they find themselves much closer to the 'mainstream' than before. Long-term communards who remember not so long ago being derided by their more conventional neighbours as hippies and freaks now receive official delegations come to inspect their ecological technologies.

This is a moment of opportunity for ecovillages. That opportunity is to dare to leave the safe niche of 'being alternative', and to enthusiastically embrace the challenge of helping mainstream society over the next several decades. For this to happen, ecovillages and local government alike need to offer the welcoming hand of friendship, the one to the other.

Resources

This section contains resources, in the form of organisations, publications, websites, videos and so on that will enable to reader to follow up on many of the initiatives and ideas discussed in this book.

Sources of information on ecovillages

The principal source of information on ecovillages is the Global Ecovillage Network, whose website is www.ecovillage.org

The GEN database providing links to ecovillage resource and events internationally is http://gen.ecovillage.org/iservices

The three regional secretariats of the Global Ecovillage Network are given below. Each has national or regional listing of all its member ecovillages.

GEN-Europe
(also with responsibility for Africa and the Middle East)

Twin offices: ZEGG and Findhorn

ZEGG, Rosa-Luxemburg-Str. 89, 14806 Belzig, Germany
Tel: (49) 33841 44766 Fax: (49) 33841 44768
http://www.gen-europe.org
Ina Meyer-Stoll ina@gen-europe.org

Findhorn Foundation, The Park, Forres, IV36 3TZ
Jonathan Dawson jonathan@gen-europe.org

(Further details of specific British ecovillages can be obtained through the Ecovillage Network of the UK: www.evnuk.org.uk)

Ecovillage Network of the Americas
For complete contact information, go to the ENA Regional Contacts webpage at http://ena.ecovillage.org/English/region

Global Ecovillage Network (Oceania &Asia)
Lot 59, Crystal Waters ecovillage, 65 Kilcoy Lane, Canondale,
Queensland 4552, Australia
Tel: (61) 75494 4741 Fax (61) 75494 4578

Max Lindegger Lindegger@gen-oceania.org
http://genoa.ecovillage.org/genoceania

Several of the ecovillages described in the text are not listed on the GEN
websites and need to be contacted independently:

The Camphill Movement
www.camphill.org or www.camphill.org.uk
Nordic Energy Folkecenter www.folkecenter.dk/en
The Hollies Ecovillage, Ireland
http://homepage.eircom.net/~thehollies

There are, in addition, a number of good directories:

S. Bunker et al (Eds.), *Diggers and Dreamers: The Guide to Communal Living (in
the UK) 2004/5*, Diggers and Dreamers Publications 2003.
www.diggersanddreamers.org.uk

Eurotopia: Directory of Intentional Communities and Ecovillages in Europe.
www.eurotopia.de or www.edgeoftime.co.uk

Nick White *(Ed.), Sustainable Housing Schemes in the UK: A Guide with Details
of Access*, Hockerton Housing Project 2002. www.hockerton.demon.co.uk

Hockerton Housing Project *The Sustainable Community: A Practical Guide*,
www.hockerton.demon.co.uk

Barbara Knudsen, *Eco-Villages and Communities in Australia and New Zealand*,
GENOA Publication ISBN 0-646-38593-3

Ecovillage-based initiatives described in the text

EDUCATION
Gaia Education
www.gaia.org/education

Gaia University
www.gaiauniversity.org

UNITAR/CIFAL
www.unitar.org/dcp

Living Routes
www.livingroutes.org

Travelling School of Life
www.zajezka.sk/doplnujuce%20dokumenty/TSoLife-Zajezka05report.rtf

Ecovillage Training Center, The Farm, US
www.thefarm.org/etc

Ecological Solutions, Crystal Waters, Australia
www.ecologicalsolutions.com.au/consulting.htm

Center for Creative Ecology, Kibbutz Lotan
www.kibbutzlotan.com/creativeEcology

Die Schule für Verständigung und Mediation (School for Communication and Mediation), Lebensgarten
www.mediation-steyerberg.de

CONSULTANCY
Ecological Solutions, Crystal Waters, Australia
www.ecologicalsolutions.com.au/consulting.htm

Ecovillage Institute

Center for Creative Ecology, Kibbutz Lotan
www.kibbutzlotan.com/creativeEcology

Centre for Scientific Research, Auroville
www.auroville.org/research/csr/csr.htm

Die Schule für Verständigung und Mediation (School for Communication and Mediation), Lebensgarten
www.mediation-steyerberg.de

ÖkoLoggia, Lebensgarten
www.oekologgia.de

BIOREGIONAL DEVELOPMENT
Sustainable Tompkins County, Itahca, US
www.sustainabletompkins.org

COLUFIFA, Senegal
www.cresp.sn/gensen/colufifa.htm
www.sip.sn/faoune/aajac/texte%20aajac.htm

Ecodyfi, Wales
www.ecodyfi.org.uk

PEACE WORK, ACTIVISM AND INTERNATIONAL SOLIDARITY
Kids to the Country, The Farm, US
www.plenty.org/KTC.htm

Bikes to Senegal
http://ide.idebanken.no/bibliotek_engelsk/ProsjektID.asp?ProsjektID=333

Plenty International, The Farm, US
www.plenty.org

PeaceRoots Alliance, The Farm, US
www.peaceroots.org

Windows: Channels for Communication, Israel
www.win-peace.org/texts/HalonotNews.pdf

Eco Center Latinovac, Croatia
www.latinovac.org

EARTH RESTORATION
Trees for Life, Findhorn
www.treesforlife.org.uk

Swan Conservation Trust, The Farm, US
www.swantrust.org

Center for Creative Ecology, Kibbutz Lotan
www.kibbutzlotan.com/creativeEcology

ORGANIC FOOD
EarthShare, Findhorn
www.earthshare.co.uk

FACILITATION & MEDIATION
International Institute for Facilitation and Consensus, Mexico
www.iifac.org

Die Schule für Verständigung und Mediation(School for Communication
and Mediation), Lebensgarten
www.mediation-steyerberg.de

Findhorn Foundation Consultancy
www.findhorn.org/connect/consultancy

PLANNING
Chapter 7, UK
www.tlio.org.uk/chapter7

OTHERS
BedZED, UK
www.bedzed.org.uk

University of Kassel study into emissions in various German communities
www.usf.uni-kassel.de/glww/texte/ergebnisse/
1bedarfsfeld0_zusammenfassung.pdf
www.usf.uni-kassel.de/usf/forschung/projekte/kaufungen.en.htm

Findhorn Foundation ecological footprint study. For details, contact the
Findhorn Foundation www.findhorn.org

Other useful organisations

International Communal Studies Association
www.ic.org/icsa/conf_2004_program.html

Utopian Studies Society, Europe
www.utopianstudieseurope.org

Fellowship of Intentional Communities (US)
www.ic.org

Federation of Egalitarian Communities (US)
www.thefec.org

Cohousing networks
UK www.cohousing.co.uk

US www.cohousing.org

Canada www.cohousing.ca

Magazines and journals
The GEN-Europe website carries many articles on ecovillages

http://gen.ecovillage.org/iservices/publications/articles.php

http://gen.ecovillage.org/iservices/publications/pm.php

Permaculture Magazine (incorporating GEN News) carries ecovillage stories in every issue

www.permaculture.co.uk

Communities (US and international)

www.ic.org/cmag/

Cohousing (US and international)

www.cohousing.org/services/journal

Books
A number of recent publications give an up-to-date picture of the current state of the ecovillage and intentional communities movement:

Jan Bang, *Ecovillages: a practical guide to sustainable communities*, Floris Books, 2005

Diana Leafe Christian, *Creating a Life Together: Practical Tools to Grow Ecovillages and Intentional Communities*, New Society Publishers, 2003

Simon Fairlie, *Low Impact Development: Planning and People in a Sustainable Countryside.* Jon Carpenter 1997.

Hildur Jackson and Karen Svensson, *Ecovillage Living: Restoring the Earth and her People*, Green Books, 2002

Graham Meltzer, *Sustainable Community: Learning from the Cohousing Model*, Trafford, 2005

Bill Metcalf, *The Findhorn Book of Community Living*, Findhorn Press, 2004

Liz Walker, *Ecovillage at Ithaca: pioneering a sustainable culture*, New Society Publications, 2005

A full bibliography for those wishing to dive deeper can be found in Bill Metcalf's Findhorn Book of Community Living.

Websites
The key portal for all seeking information on ecovillages is the GEN website: www.ecovillage.org.

Other valuable websites include:

www.evnuk.org.uk/EVNUK, the Ecovillages Network UK

www.sustainablehomes.co.uk an extremely useful database of specific cases based on answers to a detailed questionnaire

www.icdb.org database on intentional communities

www.gaia.org the foundation that started GEN

www.cohousing.org UK co-housing site

www.housingcorp.gov.uk the government social housing body, interested in community involvement

www.aecb.net Association of Environmentally Conscious Builders

www.transitionculture.org an evolving exploration of Peak Oil as an opportunity to create a sustainable society, with a strong ecovillage contribution

Videos, DVDs and other resources
Auroville: 36 Years of Research Towards a Sustainable Future (2005)
outreach@auroville.in

Crystal Waters, Permaculture Village (1999)
http://genoa.ecovillage.org/genoceania/products/index.html

Damanhur: A great adventure (2003) http://synergea.it

The Findhorn Foundation: Straight from the Heart (1995)
www.findhorn.org/store

The Future of Paradise (an Australian Planner travels to European ecovillages) (2000) michael@byronpropertysearch.com.au

Sustainable in Community (film about an academic study of CO_2 emissions in German communities) (2004)
http://www.gen-europe.org/e-shop/index.html

Visions of Utopia: Experiments in Sustainable Community (2002)
http://fic.ic.org/video

ZEGG: Presentation of a Cultural Model (1977)
ramona.stucki@t-online.de

THE SCHUMACHER SOCIETY
Promoting Human-Scale Sustainable Development

The Society was founded in 1978 after the death of economist and philosopher E.F. Schumacher, author of seminal books such as *Small is Beautiful, Good Work* and *A Guide for the Perplexed*. He sought to explain that the gigantism of modern economic and technological systems diminishes the well-being of individuals and communities, and the health of nature. His work has significantly influenced the thinking of our time.

The aims of the Schumacher Society are to:

• Help assure that ecological issues are approached, and solutions devised, as if people matter, emphasising appropriate scale in human affairs;

• Emphasise that humanity can't do things in isolation. Long term thinking and action, and connectedness to other life forms, are crucial;

• Stress holistic values, and the importance of a profound understanding of the subtle human qualities that transcend our material existence.

At the heart of the Society's work are the Schumacher Lectures, held in Bristol every year since 1978, and now also in other major cities in the UK. Our distinguished speakers, from all over the world, have included Amory Lovins, Herman Daly, Jonathon Porrit, James Lovelock, Wangari Maathai, Matthew Fox, Ivan Illich, Fritjof Capra, Arne Naess, Maneka Gandhi, James Robertson, Vandana Shiva and Zac Goldsmith.

Tangible expressions of our efforts over the last 25 years are: the Schumacher Lectures; the Schumacher Briefings; Green Books publishing house; Schumacher College at Dartington, and the Small School at Hartland, Devon. The Society, a non-profit making company, is based in Bristol and London. We receive charitable donations through the Environmental Research Association in Hartland, Devon.

Schumacher UK Members receive Schumacher Briefings, Schumacher Newsletters, discounts on tickets to Schumacher Lectures & Events and a range of discounts from other organisations within the Schumacher Circle, including Schumacher College, Resurgence Magazine and the Centre for Alternative Technology (CAT).

**The Schumacher Society, CREATE Environment Centre,
Smeaton Road, Bristol BS1 6XN Tel/Fax: 0117 903 1081
admin@schumacher.org.uk www.schumacher.org.uk**

SCHUMACHER BRIEFINGS